MEET THE DOG THAT DIDN'T SH*T

101 REFLECTIONS ON WORDS AND THEIR MAGIC

Gordon S. Jackson

Black Rose Writing | Texas

ISBN: 978-1-68433-862-7
PUBLISHED BY BLACK ROSE WRITING
www.blackrosewriting.com

Printed in the United States of America
Suggested Retail Price (SRP) $20.95

Meet the Dog that Didn't Sh*t is printed in Bookman Old Style

*As a planet-friendly publisher, Black Rose Writing does its best to eliminate unnecessary waste to reduce paper usage and energy costs, while never compromising the reading experience. As a result, the final word count vs. page count may not meet common expectations.

Praise for
MEET THE DOG THAT DIDN'T SH*T

"A joyful, light-hearted romp through a lifetime of collecting, exploring and sharing the wonderful world of words. *Meet the Dog* is laugh-out-loud funny in places and just plain fascinating in others, and you'll keep coming back to read your favorite chapters again. If you enjoy crossword puzzles, Scrabble, writing well or just knowing more than anyone else at the table, this book will be a treat!"
—Natasha Curry, medical copy editor, Cape Town

"With wit and thoroughness, Gordon Jackson takes readers on a journey through the looking glass of English words. This is an indulgent and fun exploration for lovers of language, readers and writers who understand that words do, indeed, matter. As a Canadian who has lived and traveled in places that use one variation or another of English words and phrases, I found *The Dog That Didn't Sh*t* to be not only informative, but an enjoyable holiday of sorts (or is that vacation?), the perfect book for a road trip, or a flight, or simply a quiet evening getaway."
—Thomas Froese, Columnist, *Hamilton Spectator*, Ontario

"Like a master confectioner with an endless supply of ingredients, Gordon Jackson has created a broad and irresistible selection of treats for word lovers. Select a few at a time and savor them. Put the whole lot in a bag, or a sack—or a poke, as one of my octogenarian Appalachian friends might say—and just dig in, grab a random assortment and binge. If you share Jackson's deep love of words and agree with him that they are "essential to our humanity," this book should delight

and inform you. However you choose to consume *The Dog That Didn't Sh*t*, know it will go down smoothly, evince the beauty and breadth of the English language, and leave you eager to pick around in the poke again. As we might say here in the mountains of southern Appalachia, it's fine as frog hair."
—Jeff Keeling, Reporter, WJHL TV, Johnson City, Tennessee

"Jackson uses personal experience, word knowledge, humor, and other factors that affect our communication to highlight the importance of clear communication with others. It will inform you and at times confront you with word usage clichés. It will also open the door to improving your communication. In this time of conflict, which is dividing this country, this book can be very helpful in making clear what we wish to communicate to others."
—The Rev. Carol Kirkpatrick, Pastor, Presbyterian Church (USA)

"This book sparked in me a new appreciation for words. Jackson has a way with words that makes the reader feel like a good friend who is involved in a great discussion. *Meet the Dog* will inspire the reader to use words more effectively and creatively. As a teacher, I gained a better appreciation and motivation for teaching words and their value to my students."
—Marin McInelly, high school English Language Arts teacher, Kuna, Idaho

"*Meet the Dog that Didn't Sh*t* is a diverse compilation and examination of such language constructs as clichés, oxymorons, and politically correct language use. Jackson ascribes to a precision of words, while simultaneously understanding their origins, evolutions and uses across time and varied social contexts. Throughout the book, he illuminates multiple stances towards words, some rigid and others more fluid as informed by its diverse users. Using lilting humor throughout, you will giggle, sigh, wonder, and be drawn into Jackson's orbit in his ways with words. A must read for the language savvy aficionado."
—Trish Morita-Mullaney, Ph.D., Associate Professor of Language and Literacy, Purdue University

"In his lively tribute to words and their usage, Jackson reflects on "words worth fighting for" and others "worth fighting against." Here is a compendium on topics and usages from the mind of a career journalist and professor. A must-read for all those who pursue the perfect word."
—Leah Reiter, former editor at the *International Herald Tribune* and the *Los Angeles Times*

"Gordon Jackson has written a book that is a must-read for writers, both those who are new to the craft and those who are experienced. Using his skill as a wordsmith, he has something to teach everyone about the correct use of the English language and, in this time of seemingly easy and quick writing because of computers, the importance of saying precisely what you mean. While such a book could be dull, he makes it interesting with numerous examples of correct and incorrect writing and his well-known wit. Readers will come away from this book feeling like they have been mentored by a long-time friend."
—Patrick Washburn, Professor Emeritus, E. W. Scripps School of Journalism, Ohio University.

To Winston and Noella, with gratitude.
They know why.

MEET THE DOG
THAT DIDN'T SH*T
101 REFLECTIONS ON WORDS AND THEIR MAGIC

"The words! I collected them in all shapes and sizes, and hung them like bangles in my mind."
—Hortense Calisher

"[T]here are no uninteresting words, not in English, not in Indo-European, not (I have to guess here, because of sparse acquaintance) in any of the languages in between. Not, I happily predict, in any of the three thousand or more separate languages now spoken on the planet. Every word, no exceptions, is an enchantment, a wonder, a marvel."
—Lewis Thomas

Introduction

It was 1979. I had just started graduate school at Indiana University and was chatting with my friend, a Texan. He and I shared a desk at the University's School of Journalism, as it was then known. His accent was unmistakably Texan, mine was (and is) South African. The difference required me to listen especially carefully. Also, it is important to note, his vocabulary was uncharacteristically clean for someone who had spent as long in journalism as he had.

He told me that his family had acquired a new dog. I presumably said something bland like, "That's nice." Then he announced that the dog didn't sh*t.

I knew I couldn't be hearing what I was hearing. First, I'd never heard of such a beast and if one had suddenly evolved or been genetically engineered, I thought it unlikely my desk-mate would be one of the first people to have it. Second, he didn't use words like this. I desperately needed more information. I am sure I responded with a cautious "That's interesting," or something similar.

He elaborated on how much tidier things would be as a result. Knowing how messy dogs can be and having done poop-scoop duty with our family's dogs in my youth, I affirmed how convenient that must be. His continuing comments about a dog that didn't sh*t reminded me of Sir Arthur Conan Doyle's Sherlock Holmes tale about "The Dog that Didn't Bark." But I was still no closer to bridging this gap between us, of which he was completely unaware.

It took a few more back-and-forths before I realized he was saying the dog didn't *shed*. Beside his Texan accent that threw me off track, there was a vocabulary problem: In British English, dogs *molt*, not shed.[1]

And so, as the social psychologists might say, my cognitive dissonance was—mercifully—resolved.

***

My background as a South African, who grew up speaking British English, shapes several sections in this book. But the *shed* episode embodies several main themes.

- Words have extraordinary power—to encourage, inspire, comfort, demoralize, enrage, embarrass, and so on, or in my conversation with my friend, to perplex.
- Language and standards are always in flux. For example, I wouldn't have imagined using *Meet The Dog That Didn't Sh*t* as a book title as recently as twenty years ago. Yet language usage in the United States has changed enough that one finds numerous words in print, on TV and certainly in social media that we never would have felt free to use in the past. Nor do we feel coy enough about these profanities or vulgarities that we feel compelled to use the sanitizing asterisk that we typically employed in the past, as in *sh*t*.[2]
- Misunderstanding a word can lead to possibly difficult or embarrassing situations.
- Words are worthy of close attention.
- And most importantly, the simple fact that words *matter*.

This book flows from a love of words that goes back as far as I can remember. That love has played out in my roles as a

---

[1] But we spell it correctly: *moult*.

[2] Whether you think this coarsening of language is good, bad or neither, is up to you. But it at least allowed me to come up with a title that was perhaps instrumental in pulling you this far into the book. I do know that neither my Dad nor my Mom would have approved.

reader, journalist, and author of books ranging from scholarly works to faith-related material and satirical novels.

I have been increasingly drawn over the years to the observation by Samuel Beckett that "Words are all we have." Of course, that's not literally true. We also have much else in our lives: each other, the joys of nature and the arts, perhaps our faith, and the gift of life itself. But Beckett is onto something: Words are essential to our very humanity. While some other species can communicate at sophisticated levels, nothing parallels human language and its breathtaking complexity. How can we *not* be fascinated by words, those building blocks of language? Think for a moment what it would be like to live a wordless life. It is impossible to imagine being human without words.

Meet The Dog That Didn't Sh*t is one word-lover's encounters with a range of word-related concepts, everything from **Alliteration** to **Euphemisms** to **Word Oddities** (What's the longest word? How many meanings does *set* have?), or profound questions that go to the heart of the human experience (Are there any words that rhyme with *orange*?).

The reflections are personal and random, addressing whatever topics interested me, and they are recorded here in the hope that you are as drawn to the words that make up our language as much as I am. The book, in other words, is a sheer indulgence; it is purely for fun, nothing else. It is not a reference book or a style manual. It is also not a how-to book on writing, a grammar guide or a manual for maintaining your lawn mower. The world is awash with excellent books on these topics and *Meet The Dog That Didn't Sh*t* doesn't presume to compete with them. Nor is this book an academic study, although I have tried to honor the values of good scholarship by attributing my sources where necessary and prizing truthfulness and accuracy by never knowingly hyping a topic or misleading the reader.

One other thought on the tone of the book: Given the somewhat random, or at least arbitrary, selection of topics, you may find yourself with a touch of reader's whiplash in moving from a straightforward, even earnest, topic to a lighthearted or frivolous entry right afterwards. All I can say is don't say you weren't warned.

In preparing this material I have fought the temptation to provide lengthy lists of examples. Any old fool can compile a list. But then, I like to think I am not just any old fool,[3] so I have tried to limit the lists to give enough examples to illustrate a point. Your remedy, if you think some of the lists are too long, is to skip them.

Then there is the issue of inclusive language. Some quotes[4] use "man," "mankind" and so on when referring to people in general. These quotes reflect earlier usage which characterizes contemporary English less and less. In keeping with the volume's commitment to presenting quoted material as accurately as possible, I have included these entries with their original wording. However, in a concession to the need for consistency, I have changed British spellings to American ones.

I apologize in advance for whatever errors this book undoubtedly contains. (Well, that takes care of that.)

The book's emphasis is obviously on English but we will occasionally touch on some other languages as well. As you browse this volume you'll no doubt ask why some topics close to your heart are missing. Well, as I noted previously, this is a set of personal reflections: I included the topics that interested me. But I am confident that if you are a word-nerd[5] like me you will find plenty to entertain and enrich you in the pages ahead.

---

[3] Maybe old.

[4] Some people insist on keeping the difference between *quotation*, the noun, and *quote*, the verb, and would resist my use of *quote* in this way. My background in journalistic usage explains my comfort with this approach, although the purists would say that doesn't excuse it.

[5] I am tempted to say *logophile* but we've had enough long words for now.

Acronyms

They're all around us: abbreviations that read like words, made up of the first letters of other words. Some have even become words whose heritage we don't recognize, like *scuba* and *radar* (standing for <u>S</u>elf-<u>C</u>ontained <u>U</u>nderwater <u>B</u>reathing <u>A</u>pparatus and <u>RA</u>dio <u>D</u>etection <u>A</u>nd <u>R</u>anging respectively). Here are ten more, most of which are well known but with some possible surprises.

- ABBA—The Swedish pop group, whose name was formed by taking the first letters of those in the group: Agnetha, Anni-frid, Benny and Bjorn.
- AWOL—Absent With Out Leave.
- COLA—Cost Of Living Adjustment.
- FUBAR—A military acronym, typically, standing for Fouled-Up Beyond All Recognition. At least, that's the family-friendly version.
- KISS—Keep It Simple, Stupid. Generally sound advice. See entry on **KISS**.
- NIMBY—Not In My Back Yard.
- POSH—Many people think the word stands for Port Out Starboard Home. This word merits its own entry, where you will find a supposed explanation and its debunking. See **POSH—An Awakening.**
- POTUS—President Of The United States
- QANTAS—The Australian Airline, standing for Queensland and Northern Territorial Aerial Services.
- SCOTUS—Supreme Court Of The United States.
- TLA—Three Letter Acronym[6]

---

[6] OK, OK, this is cheating. So what are you going to do about it?

***

The US military is famous for its reliance on acronyms and abbreviations. But many professions or groups develop their own vocabularies. One rich source of abbreviations is the medical world. Michael Quinion, one of Britain's premier word gurus, cites several of these:

- DNR—Do Not Resuscitate.
- CBC—Complete Blood Count.
- NPO—This is from the Latin, Nil Per Os, which means nothing by mouth, for patients who must not eat or drink for the time being.

But then Quinion lists some of the unofficial lingo, courtesy of a Dr. Adam Fox, a physician at St. Mary's Hospital in London. In a BBC interview Dr. Fox shared some of the examples of the more than 200 acronyms he had collected. Among them was TTFO—Told To [Go Away], the polite version. Called to explain this one by a patient, a quick-thinking doctor said it meant To Take Fluids Orally. Some others: FLK—Funny-Looking Kid and LOBNH—Lights On But Nobody's Home.

Another, not mentioned in the Fox interview, is the acronym GOMER: Get Out Of My Emergency Room, applied to a patient near death and taking up unnecessary space.

Alliteration

Why do companies like names such as "Bed, Bath and Beyond" or "Best Buy"? Good question, the short answer being "alliteration." We'll come back to the longer answer shortly.

But first let's define *alliteration*, which isn't nearly as gratifying as exploring it. To be clear on what we are talking about, alliteration is the repetition of a certain sound, typically a consonant, at the beginning of successive words. The saying, "Peter Piper Picked a Peck of Pickled Peppers," is an excellent and well-known example.

The key concept is that there's a repetition of sound, regardless of spelling. "Five fine photos" has the two F's and the PH letters pronounced the same. By contrast, "The changing climate..." isn't alliteration because the CH and C sounds are different.

What is there about alliteration that appeals to us? Many public speakers use it as a rhetorical device for getting attention or eliciting a certain response from their audience. The website literaryterms.net notes that alliteration is "a bold and noticeable device." Discussing alliteration in the context of poetry, where it is commonly used, the site notes that "Certain sounds can affect the mood of a poem. Alliteration can be used to give a poem a calm, smooth feeling or a loud, harsh feeling. For example, the phrase 'Singing songs of the seaside' utilizes the S sound. This gives the phrase a soft and smooth sound. Meanwhile, the phrase 'Keep that crazy cat out!' uses a hard K sound. This gives the phrase a harsh sound and adds a threatening tone." Generally, alliteration adds interest and emphasis to both written and spoken material.

Alliteration can also be helpful in memorizing material. Perhaps that's why many companies have alliterative names:

- Bed Bath & Beyond
- Best Buy
- Coca Cola
- Dunkin' Donuts
- PayPal

Think how different "Bed Bath & Beyond" would sound if the company were named "Bed, Shower & More." Far less memorable. Or "Best Buy" as "Best Purchasing"? Dull, dull, dull.[7]

An effective use of alliteration in public speaking comes in Martin Luther King's "I have a dream speech," which included this powerful sentence: "I have a dream that my four little children will one day live in a nation where they will not be judged by the color of their skin but by the content of their character."

Quite apart from its serious uses it can be just plain fun. If you're with a group of like-minded devotees, you may enjoy an occasional alliteration-fest. But be aware that alliteration can easily be overdone, to the point of annoying people.

***

A good road-trip game involves compiling an alliterative imaginary shopping list, to which each person playing has to add an item with the same sound. It would go something like this:

- First person: "On my shopping list I've got apples."
- Second person: "On my shopping list I've got apples and anchovies."

---

[7] Notice surreptitious but I hope effective intrusion of alliteration.

- Third person: "On my shopping list I've got apples, anchovies and avocadoes."
- Etc. (Presumably you don't want derivatives like "… apples and applesauce," but it's your game—you can do what you like.)

***

I feel I should finish this section with a flourish but I am floundering and failing to find something fitting.

Ambiguity

For a long while the Internet has circulated entertaining lists of ambiguous wording in letters of recommendation. Here are some examples.

- It is difficult to say enough good things about this person.
- I can assure you that no person would be better for the job.
- It would be difficult to find someone else with this person's work ethic.
- She gives every appearance of being a competent, loyal employee.
- I don't believe he could have performed better in his previous position.
- You will be fortunate if you can get this person to work for you.
- No salary would be too much for him.
- I recommend him to you with no qualifications whatsoever.

***

What's fun about these statements is the unspoken inference you will draw, which you need to fill in for yourself. Take this example: *Tonight's speaker is Mr. Arbuthnot. We could not get a better man.* (Goodness knows, we tried....)

Anagrams

Anagrams are a word puzzler's delight. The point is to reassemble the letters in a word or phrase to make another legitimate word (or phrase). But the true challenge to the wannabe anagramist is to do so in a way that logically connects with the original. We'll do no more here than pay tribute to the efforts of some creative minds.

- A decimal point = I'm a dot in place
- Endearments = tender names
- The eyes = they see
- Gold and silver = grand old evils
- A shoplifter = has to pilfer
- Softheartedness = often sheds tears

***

These days, instead of just tinkering with various arrangements of letters in the hope some sensible words will emerge, one can now seek a computer's help. Purists will undoubtedly see that as cheating. But if that doesn't bother you, one website that will generate anagrams from words up to fifteen characters long is https://word.tips/anagram-solver. Insert your name, or someone else's like your favorite or least favorite politician, and see what you get.

***

"Oh, I see we have a question. Yes, you at the back there, in the blue top. 'Is there an anagram of the word *anagram*? I'm glad you asked. It's *argaman*, which has two meanings: it's a purple dye or color, or an Israeli wine grape.

"No, I hadn't heard of it either. I looked up *anagram* in Wiktionary, which has a great feature of giving anagrams of the words it defines.

"One more question, the man up front in the red shirt: 'Is there an anagram for *argaman*, you ask?'"

Animal Adjectives

Sure, we know the words to describe "dog-like" (*canine*) and "cat-like" (*feline*). Maybe even the words regarding horses (*equine*) and fish (*piscine*). But there's a whole menagerie of other adjectives, waiting in a verbal animal shelter saying, "pick me, pick me!" As you look into one set of pleading adjectival eyes, beside you is your ten-year-old daughter urging you, "Oh please Daddy, let's take this one." Then your eight-year-old son says, "I want one too—I want that one."

So you end up going home with *lapine* (to do with rabbits) and *cricetine* (to do with hamsters). You know your wife is going to sigh and say, "Well, that's all fine and dandy" (she uses these old-fashioned expressions), but where are we going to keep all these words? And who's going to look after them? Words need to be used regularly, you know? And who will make sure they're always spelled correctly?"

The kids promise they'll take great care of their new words.

You, in turn, are glad you resisted the temptation to bring home a few more. You were especially drawn to *elephantine* (one of the few immediately recognizable ones); *lupine* (to do with wolves); *macropine* (kangaroos); *ursine* (bears); and *vulpine* (foxes).

But already you're surreptitiously planning a return trip to the shelter. You just want to browse a bit more. Maybe another visit will allow you to look a bit longer at *pardine* (leopards) and *alcelaphine* (antelope). Hmmm... that's a combination you realize may not go well together.

Baby's First Words

The website popsugar.com lists the fifteen most common first words that babies say.[8] The main reasons these words appear, the article says, are the ease of pronunciation and the frequency with which a child hears the words. For example, "Dad" typically appears sooner than "Mom" because it's easier for infants to say the D sound than an M. Based on a survey of 11,000 moms, this is what they found.

1. *Dad* (or *Dada, Daddy, Papa*, etc.)
2. *Mom* (or *Mama, Mommy, Mum*, etc.)
3. *Hi* (or *Hiya, Hey, Heya, Hello*)
4. *Buba* (or *Bub* or *Baba*)
5. *Dog* (or *Doggy, Puppy*)
6. *Ball*
7. *No*
8. *Cat* (or *Kitty*)
9. *Nana*
10. *Bye*
11. *Duck*
12. *Ta* (or *Tata*)
13. *Baby*
14. *Uh oh*
15. *Car*

***

Of course, it's not only the child who is learning from the adult. Grown-ups around young children start talking like them too.

---

[8] www.popsugar.com/family/Most-Common-First-Words-According-Moms-27331155.

There's the story of the woman during World War II who lived in the English countryside. She took care of a young family member from the city, one of thousands of children who were evacuated to the relative safety away from the bombing in the urban areas.

She spent several years with the young boy as her constant companion until the war ended, when he returned to his parents. But even newly acquired habits die hard. The woman one day found herself seated next to an elderly man on a bus, to whom she turned and, pointing out the window, said, "See the pretty choo-choo."

Borrowed Words

To say that English is to a large degree made up of borrowed words is inaccurate; English doesn't *borrow* words. It annexes them; it seizes them; it appropriates, commandeers, grabs and steals them. Like a colonial power in the old days, encountering a new piece of real estate an explorer thinks the monarch of the day would like added to the empire, English just takes what it likes and incorporates into its own vocabulary whatever her majesty's representative in a foreign territory happens to discover.

The key difference is that the "borrowed" word stays in its original language but at the same time becomes entrenched in English, which has no intention of returning it. Or, as writer James Nicoll said, "English doesn't borrow from other languages. English follows other languages down dark alleys, knocks them over and goes through their pockets for loose grammar."

That's an overstatement of "borrowing's" impact, as nothing is necessarily lost to the original language. Nevertheless, English comes away from this one-sided transaction extraordinarily enriched. According to dictionary.com, "As many as 350 other languages are represented and their linguistic contributions actually make up about 80 percent of English. Ranking from most influential to least, English is composed of words from: Latin, French, German, Italian, Spanish, Dutch, Scandinavian, Japanese, Arabic, Portuguese, Sanskrit, Russian, Maori, Hindi, Hebrew, Persian, Malay, Urdu, Irish, Afrikaans, Yiddish, Chinese, Turkish, Norwegian, Zulu, and Swahili.[9] And that's not even 10 percent of the 350 languages in the English melting pot."

English has therefore aptly been described as a mongrel language.[10] It is shameless in its seeking potentially useful additions to its always expanding vocabulary. Ralph Waldo Emerson said English is "the sea which receives its tributaries from every region under heaven." And he was writing long before English continued its rampage around a now increasingly globalized world, like a huge linguistic mega-corporation engaging in acquisitions wherever it finds them.

The fact that English has incorporated into its vocabulary words from virtually every major language helps explain why non-native speakers find it so difficult to learn English; it does not have the same level of consistency in its spelling and usage as other languages. (See for example **Ough Words**.)

Rather than offer you a long list of borrowed words, for nostalgia's sake I'll go back to my roots for two categories of examples. First, here's a selection of words and their origins, as published by a website at my alma mater, the University of Cape Town:

> *They/Their*—These common pronouns come from the Old Norse word "peir."
>
> *Person*—This comes from the Latin "persona." It was adopted into French and then made its way into English.
>
> *Very*—This despised yet commonly used adjective comes from the Old French "verai," which means "true."

---

[9] I'm puzzled to see that Greek is missing from this list. But I figure the folks at dictionary.com know more than I do. Other analyses include Greek as a major contributor.

[10] For a short but helpful description of the main contributors to English, and the types of words they brought our way, see this Wikipedia article:
https://en.wikipedia.org/wiki/Foreign_language_influences_in_English.

Dollar—This comes from Czech through Dutch. Its roots are connected to the origins of the mint itself: a factory where coins and currency is produced.

War—This comes from the Old French "were."

Leg and *Skin*—Both words come from Old Norse and replaced "shank" and "hide" upon their arrival. Although the words still exist in English, they are used only for animals once slaughtered.

Slaughter—This comes from the Old Norse "slatr."

Skipper—This comes from the Dutch "schipper." Many of our nautical terms are derived from the Dutch, who were legendary in setting up maritime trade links, especially with the east.

Court—In French this means the king's residence and was often the place to which someone was called in order to respond to accusations.

Zero—This comes from Arabic. Many of our words related to numeracy, mathematics and trade can be traced back to Arabic.

***

My second source of interest from South Africa is Afrikaans, the simplified form of the Dutch language that was the mother tongue of the early white settlers in the 1600s. It is spoken today by perhaps seven million South Africans as their first language. It too has made its contributions to English; our dictionary.com ranking places it twentieth. Here are half a dozen words you may recognize:

Aardvark—Just what you think it is.

Apartheid—The white government's policy from 1948 until the first democratic elections in 1994, it means "apart-ness" or "separate-ness." South Africans pronounce it as a-PART-hate. Americans insist on getting it wrong by saying a-part-HIDE.

Biltong—Known to Americans as jerky.
Rooibos—Literally "red bush," used as a herbal[11] tea or
    for cosmetic purposes like face wash.
Trek—An arduous journey.
Veld—Open field.

***

Just for the fun of it, you might want to open a dictionary (a real, hard-copy version) to a randomly chosen page. Then look at the origins of each of the words on the page. Some etymologies will probably be unknown but most words will be from Latin, or French or Old English. Maybe even keep a scorecard to see which category wins. Or you could just re-read this entry and save yourself the time.

***

English, as a world language, is now engaged in a reverse process: it is in turn supplying words to other languages. According to *The Boston Globe*, "English's dominance as a word exporter is a sign of its importance as an international tongue. The rate of a language's lending is one marker of its prestige," says Martin Haspelmath, a linguist at the Max Planck Institute.

Examples of English words seeping into other languages include German embracing *teenagers*, or Italian (like many other languages turning to English for technical terms) using *router* and *internet*. The Japanese are particularly skillful at incorporating a foreign word, whether from English or other languages, and massaging the pronunciation so that it sounds

---

[11] So, should this be "a herbal tea" or "an herbal tea"? Depends on how you were taught to pronounce "herbal." If you do so correctly, like me, with a hard H, good for you. If you use a soft H—actually, a non-existent H—not to worry. There's much we can do these days with good therapy to sort you out.

home grown. Examples are *sumato* (smart), *nyuu ritchi* (new rich), and *upatodatu* (up to date).[12]

Words, it appears, can develop a will of their own and travel without passports where they wish. English words dealing with popular culture, business, and technology are especially common travelers. Whereas some countries either welcome these English words or else don't care much one way or another, the French have a reputation for zealously protecting their mother tongue and resisting the dreaded Anglicisms. Well, some of them do. The French government has over the past several decades set up various committees, a recent one being the *Commissariate Général de la Langue Française* to stamp out unwanted English words. But words such as *brunch, brainstorming* and *OK* seem to have arrived, and plan to stay. So has *smartphone*, but officialdom has told the French not to use the word.

The country's language guardians are also fighting an uphill battle, as a French-teacher friend of mine noted.[13] She added that one might think that we would be borrowing all the food- and beverage-related terms from français. But the French like at least some of what we eat, she said, listing:

Le cookie
Le muffin
Le brownie
Le brunch
Le fast-food
Le chewing gum (pronounced *"shwang gum"*)
Le cocktail
Le (h)appy (h)our
　　Bon appetit!

---

[12] Several of these examples are taken from Bill Bryson's *The Mother Tongue*, which has an excellent chapter on "English as a World Language."
[13] Thanks Leslie.

British vs American English

England is a very popular foreign country to visit because the people there speak some English. Usually, however, when they get to the crucial part of a sentence they'll use words that they made up, such as "scone" and "ironmonger."
—Dave Barry

When our children were small and we turned for our babysitting needs to one of my students, the first thing to do if they were new to our family was a vocabulary lesson. We needed to define the child-related words shaped by our British English background, which seemed to some of these students to come from a different language. Here are the vital concepts these intrepid students needed to know:

- *Nappies* were *diapers.*
- The *pram* was the *stroller.*
- A *plaster* was a *band-aid.*
- A *dummy* was a *pacifier.*

One more example came from another linguistic source: Zulu. Having grown up in South Africa, my wife and I for some reason used the Zulu word for medicine: *muti.*

Some students who babysat for us went on study abroad programs to English-speaking countries. In this quite different setting, comparable vocabulary lessons were required. Well known differences between British and US English include:

- *Bonnet* vs hood of a car.
- *Boot* vs trunk of a car.

- *Braces* vs suspenders.
- *Dual carriageway* vs divided highway.
- *Flat* vs apartment.
- *Holiday* vs vacation.
- *Jug* vs pitcher.
- *Lift* vs elevator.
- *Naughts and crosses* vs ticktacktoe.
- *Pavement* vs sidewalk.
- *Petrol* vs gas or gasoline.

When leading study programs to South Africa I needed to warn my students of another difference: "Don't use the term 'fanny-pack' within hearing of South African ears." The reason: In British English "fanny" is slang for a woman's private parts.

When Winston Churchill supposedly said of the Brits and Americans that "We are divided by a common language,"[14] he overstated the reality. But the fact remains: Even people of goodwill who have these different linguistic legacies get into trouble. Our friends Colleen and Fred fit in that category; she has a British-English background and he is American. Shortly after they were married she prepared a special dinner. Hoping for warm affirmation for her cooking, she was devastated to hear Fred say the meal was "Quite nice." For him, that was high praise. "Quite," for him, meant "very, strongly, extremely." But she understood the word to mean "somewhat, all right, satisfactory, meh"—far from the praise she hoped for, and which he had intended. It took them a while to get past that moment.

It took me even longer to realize how I had not picked up on a word difference. The entry on Moist refers to my novel, *Never Say "Moist" at Wyndover College*, a satire about words banned on a college campus. Originally I wanted to title the book *Mustn't Say "Moist" at Wyndover College*. I liked the alliteration. But then my daughter, who grew up with American English, told me, "Americans don't say 'mustn't.'" She was right. I spoke

---

[14] Also attributed to Oscar Wilde and George Bernard Shaw.

with a friend who's a reference librarian, because they know everything, and she confirmed what my daughter had said. After four decades in the country, immersed in American English every day, I had somehow never noticed that this is a British usage.

This was a minor matter, though. You will find other personal wording issues in **Personal Word Blunders.**

Clichés

One of George Orwell's words of advice on writing is not to use a phrase that you're accustomed to seeing in print, unless there's a compelling reason to do so. He hated clichés and said so. His essay, titled "Politics and the English Language," which gives advice on using words well, remains a classic set of guidelines even though it was published 1946. See the separate entry (**George Orwell**) about this essay, now nearly three quarters of a century old.

Out of respect for his memory, we'll keep the list of examples below mercifully short. Then, out of further respect for Orwell, and out of respect for the English language, go through your next piece of writing ruthlessly hunting for the clichés. Think of them as your verbal equivalent of the words written on the Statue of Liberty: "Give me your tired, your poor, Your huddled masses yearning to breathe free...." See your writing as crying out for freedom, and give the Goddess of Good Writing "your tired phrases, your predictable wording, your fresh wording yearning to break free...."

And to underscore the point that clichés abound in written and spoken English, we'll cite examples beginning with an arbitrarily chosen letter, B.

- *Beat a hasty retreat.*
- *Beyond the shadow of a doubt.*
- *Bite the dust.*
- *Blazing inferno.*
- *Blessing in disguise.*
- *Blissful ignorance.*
- *Bull in a china shop.*

- *Burn the midnight oil.*
- *Burn one's bridges.*
- *Bury the hatchet.*

In brief, avoid clichés like the plague. I don't want to paint too grim a picture but in your pursuit of excellence accept that it will be an uphill battle to make your speech and writing well and truly cliché-free.[15]

---

[15] See also **Pet Peeves** for another thought on clichés.

Collective Nouns

My friend Ewan and I were once testing each other on collective nouns, listed in a reference book I somehow lost during my many moves. It was my turn to ask and the noun in question was, wait for it, "Pigs." Immediately Ewan came up with "Bay of...."[16]

The correct answer is "a *drove* of pigs." But he deserved bonus points for his creativity. *Drove*, according to Wiktionary,[17] is also the collective noun for:

- *Asses*
- *Bullocks*
- *Cattle*
- *Donkeys*
- *Goats*
- *Hares*
- *Oxen*
- *Rabbits*
- *Sheep*

If ever you're on a game show and you're asked the collective noun for some animal, and you've forgotten the list above, the odds are good that saying *drove* will be the winning answer. I

---

[16] For younger readers (or older ones who may have slept through this event), the Bay of Pigs was the term used to describe a failed US attempt to overthrow Fidel Castro and his Communist government in 1961. The failure was a major foreign policy embarrassment for President John Kennedy, who had taken office less than four months earlier.

[17] https://en.wiktionary.org/wiki/Appendix:Glossary_of_collective_nouns_by_collective_term.

was surprised to see how many animals are taken care of with that word. But I was equally surprised to see how many others I didn't know. Here's a quick sampling from Wiktionary's alphabetical list (they don't have anything listed for J or X). Most terms apply to animals.

In the interests of full disclosure, Wiktionary notes that "many of these terms are humorous and appear only in word lists" rather than in daily use. Still, you can cite these as having appeared in an online dictionary.

Ambush of widows

- *Business of ferrets*
- *Clutch of motorcyclists*
- *Draught of butlers*
- *Equivocation of politicians*
- *Flap of nuns*
- *Glitter of generals*
- *Holiness of donuts*
- *Implausibility of gnus*
- *Kaleidoscope of butterflies*
- *Labor of moles*
- *Marvel of unicorns*
- *Number of mathematicians*
- *Ostentation of peacocks*
- *Punnet of strawberries*
- *Quiver of cobras*
- *Raffle of turkeys*
- *Snarl of leopards*
- *Tumult of tubas*
- *Unkindness of ravens*
- *Venue of vultures*
- *Wedge of geese (flying in a V)*
- *Yap of chihuahuas*
- *Zeal of zebras*

***

Then there's my friend Ted, who on reading this section, asked, "What does one call a group of collective nouns?"

Common Words

The Oxford English Corpus is a huge collection of material written in English, consisting of some two billion words. Thanks to the wizardry of computer analysis, it's been possible to determine the words most frequently used in English.

And that is about the most exciting part of this entry: that they've been able to do this. The words themselves come as something of a let-down; there's nothing surprising about them. We'll list only the top ten. (Sorry; I had hoped this wouldn't be such a dull entry.) In descending order, then:

- *The*
- *Be*
- *To*
- *Of*
- *And*
- *A*
- *In*
- *That*
- *Have*
- *I*

I warned you they were predictable. What were you expecting: *butterfly, crimson, jurisprudence* and *rectangle*? No, that's it. Sorry. Now, move along please, there's nothing more to see here. You too, sir, just move along please. You too, ma'am, just move along.

Countermand My Trousers

Fans of Steven Fry, the British comedian, actor and author, may recognize this phrase. It's an excerpt from a nonsense sentence he delivered in one of the TV shows he did with his fellow Brit, Hugh Laurie, in their 1980s programs titled *A Bit of Fry and Laurie.* In this sketch Fry riffs on the wonderful richness of English, and says: "Our language ... our language, hundreds of thousands of available words, frillions of possible legitimate new ideas, so that I can say this sentence and be confident it has never been uttered before in the history of human communication: 'Hold the newsreader's nose squarely, waiter, or friendly milk will countermand my trousers.' One sentence, common words, but never before placed in that order."

Absolute gibberish, but a perfectly grammatical sentence that proves his point: English offers a seemingly infinite set of ways to convey ideas or thoughts—not necessarily important or, in this case, even intelligible. But Fry makes a crucially important point, echoed by Simon Kirby, an academic at the University of Edinburgh who studies the origins of language. He says: "One of the really striking things about human language is that we are able to talk about things that we've never talked about before." A century ago, for example, we couldn't have had conversations about TV or the Internet, or more abstract issues like post-modernism or critical race theory.

Most of our speech, though, is mundane, as Fry parodies in the sketch: "... all of us spend our days saying the same things to each other, time after weary time ...: 'I love you,' 'Don't go in there,' 'You have no right to say that,' 'Shut up.' 'I'm hungry,' 'That hurt,' 'Why should I?,' 'It's not my fault,' 'Help,' 'Marjorie is dead.'"

Not all our speech (or writing) is so prosaic. We are blessed too with astonishing richness of word use by our best novelists and poets, journalists and playwrights, and in our more gifted public speakers—individuals who make our language sing. Even the rest of us, though, engage in an act of powerful linguistic alchemy each time we string together a cluster of words selected from our vocabularies to make a new message, quite possibly words that we've never previously used in that sequence. It's a power that rises to the level of magical. Yet day by day, we speak and write, creating one sentence after another, seldom if ever reflecting on the astonishing creativity in which we're engaged.

For the fun of it, if you have fifteen minutes to spare get a dictionary and turn to the pages that define the nine key words in Fry's sentence:
Hold/newsreader/nose/squarely/waiter/friendly/milk/countermand/trousers. Then choose any other word on each of those pages and string them together in a sentence of your own. Use the new words in any order. The result may be sheer nonsense but your sentence will quite likely never have been crafted before. Never.

***

Your fifteen minutes are probably up. But as you move on, maybe you will marvel at what those nine new words have enabled you to do.[18]

---

[18] And spare a thought for the loved ones poor Marjorie has left behind.

Crossword Puzzle Words

What's a four-letter city in Czechoslovakia? (Set aside for the moment that Czechoslovakia no longer exists; it's now divided between the Czech Republic and Slovakia.[19]) But back to the question: If you're an inveterate crossword puzzler, this is an easy one: The answer is Oslo. Get it?[20]

Writing about what he terms Crosswordese, a vocabulary little used outside the world of crossword puzzles, Paul Dickson says these words "are usually short, vowely, and obscure." He cites Eugene T. Maleska, formerly the crossword puzzle editor of *The New York Times*, as saying, "Who cares that an *anoa* is a Celebes ox, a *moa* is an extinct bird, or an *Abo* is a member of an Australian tribe?"

It takes a special kind of mind to anticipate what the creator of the puzzle is thinking. Some clues are easy but the more ingenious ones require a willingness to think laterally. Try these on for size. Answers below.

1. Black and white set. (5 letters)
2. Bouncer's place. (10 letters)
3. Break one's word. (9 letters)
4. Browning pieces. (8 letters)
5. Dame's introduction. (5 letters)
6. Grace period. (8 letters)
7. Heartless one? (6 letters)
8. It can help you get a date? (6 letters)
9. One can't do this. (4 letters)
10. One ordered to take two tablets. (5 letters)

---

[19] The country peacefully split in two on January 1, 1993.
[20] CzechOSLOvakia

11. Ones who never think of flying? (10 letters)
12. Ring bearer. (6 letters)

And the answers:

1. Chess
2. Trampoline
3. Hyphenate
4. Toasters
5. Notre
6. Mealtime
7. Tin man
8. Carbon
9. Duet
10. Moses
11. Autopilots
12. Saturn

The Desert Island Bookshelf

Let's assume I am approached by two men in dark suits, wearing dark glasses, who have driven to my front door in one of those black government-issue SUVs. They tell me they're from a highly secret government agency and that I will for reasons of national security be placed on a desert island for a year. I leave tomorrow.

"But..." I begin, thinking of my participation in the regional Morris Dancing Championships this weekend.

"No buts," the shorter of the two men (6 foot 4), tells me. "Be ready at 8 a.m. tomorrow, when an agent will escort you to the helicopter."

"Can I bring my books about words?" I ask.

"Bring whatever you like," says the taller one. "But no pepper spray, no laser pointy things, no avocados."

"Why not avocados?"

"National security; we can't tell you why. One other thing: you'll have everything you need but there'll be no Internet or any other communications with the rest of the world."

***

They leave and I realize I have the rest of the day to sort out my life. I need to contact my insurance broker, stock broker, and pawn broker; let my family know I'll be late for dinner (very, very late); get several back-up pairs of reading glasses; and put a hold on my mail. Then I begin preparing my list of books[21] to bring:

---

[21] Many of these are dated. No matter; they're my friends and I am not leaving them behind.

- *Associated Press Style Guide*—I used to tell my journalism students, for whom this was a required text, that if ever I stopped teaching I'd still hang onto this volume. (I did, and I do.) It is packed with guidance on issues you didn't even know were issues. It also has a helpful section on punctuation, to which I turn when I need to check yet again whether it is *Moses' encounter with God* or *Moses's encounter with God*. (The first option is correct.)
- *Bernstein's Reverse Dictionary*, by Theodore Bernstein. Exactly what it sounds like: you know the meaning but don't know the word. Let's say you know there's a word to describe a man who's filthy rich but can't recall it. You look up "rich man" and there's your answer: *Croesus*.
- *Chambers Dictionary*—This English dictionary is understandably overshadowed by the *Oxford English Dictionary* and *Merriam-Webster's*. A small part of my motivation for selecting this dictionary over the other two is rooting for the underdog. Admittedly, another reason would be a certain pandering to exclusivity; if there's going to be anyone else on the island (the government heavies didn't make this clear) who wants to consult a dictionary, I think that Chambers' lesser-known status would give it a certain cachet. But the most important reason is that it's an excellent dictionary, often giving me clarity that I find lacking elsewhere or including more obscure words common in Britain. You'd need to take all twenty-four volumes of the OED to compete. Yet another reason is the compilers' readiness to be playful, inserting a humorous definition every so often. Two examples: "*éclair*—a cake, long in shape but short in duration," and "*middle-aged*—between youth and old age, variously reckoned to suit the reckoner."
- *Chambers Dictionary of Quotations*—Although not strictly a words-only book, this masterful anthology shows what people through the ages have done with

words, conveying the widest imaginable array of comments and insights.

- *Dickson's Word Treasury*—A friend introduced me to this gem many years ago and lent me her copy. I immediately ordered my own. The edition I have is copyrighted 1992. Paul Dickson is an inveterate collector of words. His scope of interests is captured in what is indeed a word treasury, with entries ranging from what he claims is a record 2,660 synonyms for being drunk to forty-seven terms about hardware. Examples? The more familiar term *Allen wrench*, an L-shaped tool for locking screws and set-screws, to the far more obscure *snath*, which is the handle of a scythe (a scythe is only the blade). He even has a section on words he has made up, such as *nork*—a product that looks appealing but loses all appeal soon after you get it.
- *Dictionary of Foreign Terms,* ed. Mario Pei and Salvatore Ramondino. Just what it sounds like. Admittedly, more than most of these other reference tools, this one has been made redundant by Google. Still, it's been a good friend over the years and it's coming along.
- *Merriam-Webster's Concise Dictionary of English Usage*—Many people want their dictionary to tell them what's *right*, damn it. But instead of being prescriptive, this volume is descriptive and captures how people actually use the language, supplemented with comments from language gurus. Perhaps you are unsure if you should use *hopefully* in this sense: "He is, hopefully, now fully recovered." This guide will give you plenty of background and then let you decide for yourself. This dictionary's conclusion on *hopefully*? "You can use it if you need it or avoid it if you do not like it. There never was anything wrong with it." [Pause for angry objections....]
- *Roget's Thesaurus*—The definitive, numero uno tool for finding synonyms. This one's so important that it gets its own entry. See **Thesaurus**.

- *The Meaning of Liff*—Also in a category of its own, this slim volume by Douglas Adams and John Lloyd is an unending source of amusement as one repeatedly encounters their rich humor and inventiveness. See **The Meaning of Liff** for a fuller account of this book's merits.

- *The Meaning of Tingo: Adam Jacot de Boinod*—This fascinating book consists of words from dozens of non-English languages. These words convey an unimaginably diverse range of concepts that make you realize that even English, in all its richness, doesn't cover *everything*. Two examples: The title word, *tingo*, is in the Pascuense language from Easter Island. It means "to take all the objects one desires from the house of friend, one at a time, by borrowing them." Example no. 2: A German word, *krawattenmuffel*, meaning "one who doesn't like wearing ties." ("Oh come on, can't we have one more?" "Very well....") Example no. 3: *mokita*, from the Kiriwana language in Papua New Guinea; it means "the truth that all know but no one talks about." Surely we could find a place for this word at family gatherings?

- *The Penguin Dictionary of Curious and Interesting Words*, by George Stone Saussy III. If you pride yourself on your extensive vocabulary, a few minutes browsing through this collection is guaranteed to humble you. Well, if not you, almost all of us. (Maybe not George Stone Saussy III.) Two examples: *anorchid*, noun meaning "one without testicles," and *lapidate*, a verb meaning "to throw rocks at."

Dictionaries

Periculosum est definire. [It is dangerous to make definitions.]
   —*Latin saying*

The only thing you need to take from this entry is this: Go and read Kori Stamper's book, *Word By Word*. She's an editor at Merriam-Webster, the premier dictionary publisher in the United States. She recounts how she was drawn to the world of words and secured her dream job. Then she takes us into the heart of the dictionary-making process, the painstaking and time-consuming task of collecting example after example of how words appear in every conceivable setting: newspapers, magazines, books, ads, billboards, packaging of products, *anything*, it seems where people have placed words.

More importantly, though, she addresses head on the perpetually thorny question about the role of dictionaries. Should they be prescriptive, setting the rules and standards for those using the words a dictionary defines? In other words, should they be the protectors of our language? Or should they be descriptive, primarily telling us how words are in fact used? Stamper comes down on the second role.

That's why she gained national attention for her defense of the word *irregardless*, to which she devotes an entire chapter in the book. Even though she speaks out against the word, and its illogical meaning, the reality is that people use it. That means the dictionary cannot ignore it.

Another controversial example: Merriam-Webster decided to redefine *marriage* in 2003 to include same-sex unions. A review of Stamper's book in *The Atlantic* said, "The new definition provoked a write-in campaign to Merriam-Webster, accusing the dictionary of politics-via-lexicon. The anger was extremely predictable. Because ... words are not merely words, and not merely tools. They are intimate. They are extensions of ourselves. They are one of the few immediate ways we have to take that small piece of reality that is ours—the mind, the self, the soul, choose whichever word in the dictionary seems most apt to you—and offer it to other people."

Just as English is a dynamic and fluid language, so too must dictionaries reflect its non-static character. Dictionaries do this both by adding new words (*laser*[22] and *laptop* didn't exist a century ago) and updating the meanings we users accord existing ones.

Yet those of us who strive for and cherish "good" or what's termed "standard" English, however we define that, still seek dictionaries' support in our quest. As a minimum, we would want a dictionary to indicate that using a word like *irregardless* is problematic. In this case, thankfully, Merriam-Webster does just that. Its on-line dictionary poses the question, "Is *irregardless* a word?" Here is its answer: "Yes. It may not be a word that you like, or a word that you would use in a term paper, but *irregardless* certainly is a word. It has been in use for well over 200 years, employed by a large number of people across a wide geographic range and with a consistent meaning. That is why we, and well-nigh every other dictionary of modern English, define this word. Remember that a definition is not an endorsement of a word's use."

***

Lewis Carroll[23] was a mathematician who also knew a thing or two about words and how to use them, as he did playfully in *Alice in Wonderland* and *Through the Looking Glass*. At one point he has this exchange:

---

[22] *Laser* is an acronym for Light Amplification by Stimulated Emission of Radiation.
[23] The pen name of Charles Dodgson.

"When I use a word," Humpty Dumpty said, *in rather a scornful tone, "it means just what I choose it to mean—neither more nor less."*

"The question is," said Alice, *"whether you can make words mean so many different things."*

"The question is," said Humpty Dumpty, *"which is to be master—that's all."*

We do well to remember that regardless of Humpty Dumpty's egocentric approach to defining words, Carroll poses a profound question: Which is to be master, the words or its users?

While making definitions may be dangerous, as the Latin saying above warned us, we desperately need the clarity that dictionaries provide. Certainly, we acknowledge that definitions slowly evolve and change, sometimes 180 degrees over time. But a world without the common ground that dictionary definitions provide would be infinitely more dangerous.

Eggcorns

Merriam-Webster defines an eggcorn as "a word or phrase that is mistakenly used for another word or phrase because it sounds similar and seems logical or plausible." For example, instead of saying *take for granted*, someone may hear it as, and then repeat, *take for granite*. It makes sense: You're taking something that's grounded on solid rock. Of course, it means something different but it made sense to *you*.

Example time:

- For *all intents and purposes* becomes for *all intensive purposes*.
- *Biding my time* becomes *biting my time*.
- *Dog-eat-dog world* becomes *doggy-dog world*.
- *On the spur of the moment* becomes *on the spurt of the moment*.
- *Praying mantis* becomes *preying mantis*.

One of my favorites is *Heimlich remover* instead of *Heimlich maneuver*. Makes perfect sense: You're trying to remove whatever is causing someone to choke.

If you're bored on a rainy afternoon, dip into this website for an amusing browse: https://eggcorns.lascribe.net/browse-eggcorns/. It currently lists more than 600 eggcorns and has thoughtful comments and analysis as well.

Emperors Without Clothes

A controversy erupted in the serene halls of academe in 1996 when a physicist named Alan Sokal submitted as a hoax a paper steeped in leftist academic jargon to a journal titled *Social Text*. It was titled "Transgressing the Boundaries: Toward a Transformative Hermeneutics of Quantum Gravity." The editors accepted it for publication, without suspecting he was parodying them and their publication.

A writer in the English newspaper, *The Guardian*, said, "The article is a masterpiece of foggy prose. In it, Sokal claimed Jacques Lacan's psychoanalytic speculations had been confirmed by recent work in quantum field theory. He suggested that the axiom of equality in mathematical set theory was analogous to the homonymous concept in feminist politics. He employed scientific and mathematical concepts in ways that even an A-level student should have spotted as rubbish, but crammed the article with nonsensical—but authentic—quotes about physics and mathematics, by prominent French and American postmodern intellectuals."

The ensuing debate included charges that Sokal had acted unethically by deceiving the editors; that the journal lacked intellectual rigor; and that, as the physicist put it, the journal was willing to "publish an article liberally salted with nonsense if (a) it sounded good and (b) it flattered the editors' ideological preconceptions."

***

Now, three disclaimers. My knowledge of physics is limited to the theory of gravity: If I slip on the ice, I go down. Second, I concede that every discipline, like physics, needs its own highly specialized vocabulary.[24] Just because the language has terms unfamiliar to those outside the guild doesn't make it worthy of condemnation. And third, building on these first two points, I don't pretend to understand Sokal's piece—either the arguments he makes or the numerous gibes and inside jokes that only someone with a background in physics and mathematics could grasp.

Yet there is one important point to be made: In our use of words we need to be as clear and as concrete as possible. For decades, people have had fun satirizing users of vague, abstract language through "phrase generators." You come up with two columns of abstract-sound adjectives, and a third column of equally abstract nouns. Let's say you have ten words in each column. All you need now is a random three-digit number to generate your impressive sounding phrase that is, in the word of *The Guardian* writer cited above, just plain rubbish.

Let's begin:

Column 1 (Adjective)	Column 2 (Adjective)	Column 3 (Noun)
1. Substantial	Contributary	Projection
2. Reversible	Exponential	Turbulence
3. Gradual	Recessive	Affinity
4. Inductive	Digital	Sufficiency
5. Intransigent	Imitative	Extension
6. Global	Expansive	Diffusion
7. Compatible	Universal	Homogeneity
8. Defunctionalized	Dynamic	Phase
9. Inherent	Complementary	Polarity
10. Synchronous	Aggregating	Negativity

---

[24] So does the world of academe. Before I began my graduate work in the USA I had no idea what credit hours or a GPA were.

Let's start with 1-2-3. That gives us a "Substantial Exponential Affinity." Or 4-9-6: An "Inductive Complementary Diffusion."

Now it's over to you, to find the right occasion to inject these meaningless bits of gobbledygook into an earnest discussion, in a way that earns you admiration for your ability to see the complexity facing your organization in a fresh and penetrating way.

Admittedly, this particular set of words may not match the jargon in your workplace or sphere of activity. Replace them with vague words that will be familiar to your listeners or readers. Be prepared, though, for someone who has the temerity to suggest you don't know what you're talking about. Then you have as a ready response a 9-5-10 (an Inherent Imitative Negativity) at your disposal. This phrase, said with the right tone of superiority, will dismiss anyone who implies the Emperor has no clothes.

Epitaphs

What makes these messages special is that they serve as an ultra-condensed obituary, the last words said about a person. Most are fond, loving assessments of a person's life, typically positive but entirely predictable words like "Here lies Mary McIntyre, beloved wife and mother," followed by her birth and death dates.

Some, though, can be unexpected. Here are four examples:

For Anna:
    The children of Israel wanted bread,
    The Lord, He sent them manna.
    This poor man wanted a wife
    And the devil sent him Anna.

Les Moore, for some punning on a tombstone in, yes, Tombstone, Arizona:
    Here lies Les Moore.
    Four slugs from a .44.
    No Les.
    No More.

And two in the That's-Not-Exactly-What-We-Meant category, James Brush, dated 1831, from a Woolich churchyard in England:
    Sacred to the memory of
    Major James Brush
    Who was killed by the accidental discharge of a pistol by his orderly
    14th April 1831

Well done
Good and faithful servant.

John McFarlane, undated, from Edinburgh, Scotland:
Erected to the memory of
John McFarlane
Drowned in the Water of Leith
By a few affectionate friends.

Eponymous Words

A sizeable number of English words are based on people whose contribution to humankind was in some way noteworthy enough that their legacy, for good or ill, is perpetuated in our daily speech. An eponym, then, is a word formed from someone's name.

Some are so familiar that you can guess at their origins, such as *guillotine* and *pasteurize*. These and many others are in everyday use, such as *boycott*, *diesel*, and *sandwich*.

Captain Charles Boycott was an Englishman serving as a land agent during tough economic times in Ireland. His conduct led people to shun him for his actions in evicting farmers. His workers stopped working on his estate and his house and local businessmen refused to deal with him. Boycott has now made its way into at least seventeen other languages.[25]

Rudolph Diesel left a more positive legacy: those fuel-efficient engines that power cars, trucks, locomotives and other machinery.

John Montagu, the Fourth Earl of Sandwich was, among other things, an inveterate gambler. Not wanting to interrupt his card playing when hungry, he had a servant bring him what we know today as a sandwich, with meat between two slices of bread. This allowed him to keep playing, without using a fork or getting the cards greasy.

Each of these stories could be expanded on, as could the histories behind the other half dozen listed here. I have purposefully chosen ones that are immediately recognizable as eponyms. Included are the briefest of explanations.

---

[25] For more on Boycott and many other eponyms, look for John Bemelman Marciano's book, *Anonyponymous: The Forgotten People Behind Everyday Words.*

- *Bloomers*, from Amelia Bloomer, an early suffragette and temperance advocate, who also worked to change women's clothing styles. She didn't devise what we now know as bloomers—defined by Merriam-Webster as "full loose trousers gathered at the knee formerly worn by women for athletics" and "underpants of similar design worn chiefly by girls and women." Nevertheless this style became associated with her.
- *Dunce*, from medieval scholar and theologian John Duns Scotus. His scholarly followers became known as Dunsmen, who developed a reputation for refusing to learn any new or different ideas. Their opponents called them dunces, a severe insult to men of letters.
- *Leotard*, from Jules Léotard, a Parisian acrobat and trapeze artist, who inspired the 1867 song, "The Daring Young Man on the Flying Trapeze."
- *Mentor*, named after Mentor, who tutored Odysseus' son Telemechus while Daddy was away on his adventures.
- *Quisling*, from a Norwegian traitor in World War II, Vidkun Quisling, who was a military officer and Nazi collaborator. He was executed by firing squad in 1945.
- *Shrapnel*, from Henry Shrapnel, a lieutenant in the British Royal Navy, who invented an exploding cannon ball.

***

If this entry has whetted your appetite for more, turn to the entries on **Goldwynisms**, **Malapropisms** and **Spoonerisms**.

Errors Lists

The "errors list" is a teaching tool I stole from a colleague who taught writing.[26] I'd require my students two or three times a semester to hand in a list of mistakes they made. I emphasized in class and in the syllabus that I welcomed mistakes; that was crucial to their learning. But I insisted they make new mistakes. It's dumb to keep making the same mistake, over and over.

Here's a blend of the common errors my students made, with some that I too have made over the years. I'll leave you to speculate on which were theirs and which were mine. After exploring these take a trip to **The *Right* Word** and **Tricky Words**, to see more snares in the world of English.

- *A lot*—not "alot."
- *Affect/Effect*—*Affect* is a verb. "The drought will *affect* the farmers." *Effect* is the noun. "The drought had a devastating *effect* on the farmers." Occasionally *effect* is used as a verb, to indicate change: "The new manager *effected* numerous changes." Finally, *affect* can be used as a noun, but only in a specialized sense regarding feelings or emotions: "The accused showed no *affect* when the charges were read."
- *Could have/Could of/Could've*—The middle one is a no-no.
- *Its/It's/Its'*—*Its* is possessive; just like *his* or *hers*, it ends in an S. "The cat played with *its* ball." *It's* is a contraction of it is. "*It's* time we set the tent on fire." *Its'* does not exist. Stomp on it every time you see it.

---

[26] Thanks Jim.

Approach people in the street and correct them. Speak up in church and city council meetings to help stop this scourge. Even if others won't, I will thank you.

- *Lay/Lie*—This one's tricky enough to merit its own entry. See **Lay and Lie**.
- *Principle/Principal*—The easy way to remember this is that the *principal* is a person (although some survivors of boarding school may doubt this). The *principal*, therefore, is my *pal*.
- *Sight/Site/Cite*—*Sight* is seeing. *Site* is a location (like a website). *Cite* is what a police officer might do if he catches you doing 87 in a 25 zone.
- *Than/Then*—There is no logical reason for a speaker of British English to write "It is later then you think." Nothing except a typo can explain this error. Yet American students make this mistake repeatedly. My theory is that it's related to US pronunciation and how the word is said differently on each side of the Atlantic.
- *Their/There/They're*—The students left *their* books right *there* next to the spittoon and *they're* coming back later to get them.
- *Unique*—Some students struggle to understand that "unique" means one of a kind; something can't be more or less unique. Like being pregnant or dead.
- *Who/Whom*—Tricky enough to warrant it's own entry. See **Who/Whom**. But before you do, ask yourself: did you catch the error in the previous line? If not, go back to the *Its/It's/Its'* entry above. (Got to watch for these things, you know.) If you caught it first time, phone this book's publisher for your prize.[27]

---

[27] They're experiencing an unusually high call volume so be prepared for a long wait, I'm afraid.

- *Your/You're*—*Your* (or yours) is a simple possessive. "Is this *your* llama?" By contrast, *you're* is short for *you are* or *you were*. "I thought you said *you're* going to Louisville tomorrow."

Eschew Obfuscation

This admonition is packed with one reward after another. To begin with, *eschew*, meaning "shun" or "avoid," is a quaint, charming verb that is clearly heading to toward archaic status and might already be only one or two bus stops away. When did you last hear anyone use *eschew* in conversation or writing? It's the sort of word Charles Dickens or Jane Austen may have used. Still, it's a treat to see it in use in this context. If nothing else, it at least reminds us that it is still around.

Then we have *obfuscation*, which means to "confuse" or "make obscure." Putting the two words together, we have "be clear"—exactly the opposite of our first impression of this pretentious combination, resulting in a delightfully self-contradictory exercise in wordplay.

If it were a wine, its dominant flavor would be self-parody, with a hint of oak supplemented by overtones of mulberry and irony. Highly recommended to accompany venison or lamb.

Euphemisms

Euphemisms are unpleasant truths wearing diplomatic cologne.
  —Quentin Crisp

During my graduate school days I had a friend who, when she was heading to the restroom, would announce that she was going "to the euphemism." It was a nice recognition of the fact that whatever other term she might have used would itself have been a euphemism.

She was highlighting the very nature of this linguistic phenomenon: Euphemisms are attempts to protect us from something awkward, unpleasant or otherwise difficult to address head on. Death, sex, bodily functions, conditions like drunkenness, government blunders, business incompetence and military mistakes are some of the more common arenas where we see Quentin Crisp's quotation at work. Take death. It appears people no longer die; they pass on, join the angels, go to their heavenly home, succumb, rest in peace, or slip away. Somehow these words or phrases are supposed to make this ultimate taboo easier to face.

People don't have sex; they "sleep together"—wording that would puzzle a young child who has not yet been taught about the birds and the bees, as we delicately refer to reproduction. And "reproduction" itself points to one approach we take in our quest for euphemisms: We go scientific or technical. If you're a doctor testifying in court or writing up a medical report, you'll speak about *urine* and *feces*. If you're a Mom of a toddler, you'll use baby-talk, like *wee-wee* or *poo*. And if you're an adult, in polite company on a visit to friends, you'll probably avoid any direct reference to whatever excretory function lies in your immediate future. You'll probably just ask, "Where's your *restroom/bathroom/john/little boys' room?*" or something similar. It seems that adults are left with only three options in dealing with this topic: We go technical, use children's language, or use polite but still evasive terminology.

Being drunk is a condition that lends itself to an abundance of euphemisms. Paul Dickson, in his masterful anthology of all kinds of words, *Dickson's Word Treasury*,[28] proudly displays what he believes is a record collection of 2,660 words and phrases to describe inebriation.

More institutional euphemisms emerge from agencies like governments, the military, and the world of business. One of the best-known euphemisms from the world of government came at the end of World War II, when Japan's Emperor Hirohito surrendered—his country in tatters, with three million people dead, and Hiroshima and Nagasaki destroyed by atomic bombs: "The war situation has developed not necessarily to Japan's advantage."

Many euphemisms in government and politics deal with truth-telling. In 1906 Winston Churchill originated the phrase *terminological inexactitude* as a circumlocution for either an outright lie or else a statement that wasn't technically true.

More recently, Hillary Clinton said in 2008 that she had been pinned down on a visit to war-torn Bosnia. But video footage showed this wasn't the case and, forced to retract her statement, she said, "I did *mis-speak* the other day."

The Trump era brought us a new gem, *alternative facts*. Asked to respond to a brazen lie by President Trump's press secretary, Sean Spicer, about the size of the crowd attend Trump's inauguration in January 2017, one of the president's senior counselors, Kellyanne Conway, said Spicer was giving *alternative facts*.

Budget deficits get termed *investments* in a rosier future; budget cuts are referred to as *savings*.

---

[28] See more about this book in **The Desert Island Bookshelf**.

The world of the military, especially during Vietnam and more recently in response to 9-11, has brought us terms like *collateral damage, extraordinary rendition, armed intervention,* and *friendly fire.* Put more bluntly, these translate into, "We ended up killing a bunch of civilians," "We illegally entered another country to kidnap someone we'd like to talk to," "We attacked with lethal force," and "Oops—we ended up killing one of our own." Key enemy figures are no longer assassinated, they are *liquidated.*

In the business world people no longer get fired; they are *let go* or *made redundant.* Or the staff is being *right-sized.* Or, sadly, you could be a victim of a *workforce imbalance correction.* Cars are not second-hand or used, they're *pre-owned.* Also, in business circles it's impolite to talk about *pay* so we refer instead to *compensation* or *remuneration.* In a job interview for that entry-level job in marketing, you're unlikely to ask, "How much will you pay me?" Far better to say, "If I'm your successful candidate, what will the compensation package look like?"

The airlines have their own special vocabulary of euphemisms. The late comedian George Carlin poked fun at these, noting for example that "the unlikely event of a water landing" meant a crash.[29] And he said, "Here's a phrase that apparently the airlines simply made up: 'near miss.' They say that if two planes nearly collide that it's a near miss.... It's a near hit! A collision is a near miss."

Other examples:

---

[29] Captain Sully Sullenberger's landing of US Airways flight 1549 on New York's Hudson river in 2009, in which no lives were lost, took some of the sting out of Carlin's joke. Sullenberger and his co-pilot glided flight US 1549 to landing on New York's Hudson River on January 15, 2009, following a bird strike that killed all the plane's engines. A National Transportation Safety Board official called it "the most successful ditching in aviation history."

- People are no longer broke but have "a temporary negative cash flow."
- People no longer live in slums but "in substandard housing."
- People are no longer unemployed but "between jobs."
- People are no longer poor but are "economically disadvantaged."
- People who lie are "economical with the truth."

There's considerable overlap between euphemisms and **Political Correctness**. The intent in each category is to soften potential pain or embarrassment. Political Correctness, however, is typically rooted in more ideological thinking.

We all use euphemisms. A key to doing so is to remember the importance of tone. If you have to break bad news to someone, for example that a family member has died, you'd be ill-advised to say, "I'm sorry to tell you but Harry has kicked the bucket." It's impossible to imagine a police officer or a chaplain coming to your door and using such flippant language. Nor is it likely the official would tell you that Harry had passed on to glory. In some cases directness may be best: "I'm sorry to have to tell you that your brother Harry has died in a car accident."

The Economist magazine, in a survey of euphemistic styles around the world, said "The British are probably the world champions of euphemism. The best of these are widely understood (at least among natives), creating a pleasant sense of complicity between the euphemist and his audience."

The article continued: "British newspaper obituaries are a rich seam: nobody likes to speak ill of the dead, yet many enjoy a hint of the truth about the person who has 'passed away.' A drunkard will be described as 'convivial' or 'cheery.' Unbearably garrulous is 'sociable' or the dread 'ebullient'...."

The article concludes by warning against politically correct euphemisms, which it says "are among the most pernicious.

Good and bad become 'appropriate' or 'inappropriate.'... But euphemisms can also be benign, even necessary. Sometimes the need to prevent hurt feelings justifiably takes precedence over clarity. Saying that dim or disruptive children have 'special needs,' or that they exhibit 'challenging behavior,' does not make them easier to teach—but it may prevent them from being teased or disheartened."

Family Vocabularies

Your family, like every other family, has a language of its own, consisting of unintelligible catch phrases, favorite but not generally known quotations, obscure illusions, and well-tried, but not intrinsically humorous family jokes.
—A. A. Milne

Every family has its own vocabulary. They're shaped by a set of unique experiences each family member brings to the table, and especially those experiences the family has had together. It may be some badly pronounced word by one of the children when she was a toddler. Or it could be some mistake that Grandpa made which got immortalized in a single word, which everyone in the family knows refers to his memorable error— and which is now assured of immortality.

Or it may be your family's unique words for things like the bathroom and what happens there. Our family's vocabulary was shaped by our background in British English, so we speak of going to the *loo*. (See **British vs American English** for more examples, especially regarding our babysitting translation lesson.) Your family's regional heritage may shape your word choices for something as simple as a Coke, or its generic equivalent: Is it a *coke* (lower case C), a *soda*, a *pop*, or whatever? Yours may be the only family in your neighborhood using a particular term, one that may require interpretation when little Johnny from next door comes to play.

Other influences in your family vocab could be from the world of entertainment. Following the examples of sketches we saw in *A Bit of Fry and Laurie*, a BBC TV comedy series featuring Steven Fry and Hugh Laurie, we'll often mimic Steven Fry and stutter the word b-b-b-book, or huff and puff our way through the word "reader" in a way that's impossible to convey to print. Then, the word "excellent" took on an M at the beginning, so it's become "mexcellent"—for reasons long forgotten.

Our South African background means we also have incorporated several Afrikaans words, Afrikaans being a simplified form of Dutch and one of the country's eleven official languages. So it is that we never barbecue; we only *braai*. Occasionally, something is *lekker* (nice/pleasant) or we might swat a *miggie* (or *muggie*), a small flying insect, or deal with a *gogga*—a small bug. The G or GG sound in each of these words is guttural, like the end of *loch*.

"Morning" gets special treatment too, also in a way one cannot capture in print. It derives from an eccentric teacher my wife had in boarding school in South Africa. She greeted the girls each day by saying "morning" with a bizarre nasal twang and elongating the second syllable, sounding something like "Mornannnnnggggg." She said the word so distinctively and intriguingly that all the girls prided themselves on how well they could mimic her. Even today, half a century later, any reunion of two or more of these women always commences with a round of this mimicked greeting, accompanied by joyous laughter. In our family, my wife is the acknowledged "morning" maestro, although the rest of us will try to mimic the mimicker.

Just as words bond common language speakers together in profound ways, so too does your family vocabulary reinforce the common experiences you've had. My guess is that these are either positive experiences, or negative ones that can now be laughed at in hindsight. Take a moment over dinner tonight to identify some words unique to your family—and give thanks for the role they play in making you who you are.

Famous Last Words

We get only one shot at the last words we'll say just before death. Given the circumstances, we can hardly be certain that the examples given here are accurate statements that were said by these prominent figures. That is because many people lose coherence toward the end and are unlikely to utter the kind of memorable sayings listed below.

So, are these accurate accounts of reality, or are they more mythical versions of what people said on their deathbed? Or perhaps these things were said toward the end of their lives and whatever other utterances that followed weren't as quotable. And how reliable was the person who supposedly heard, and then transcribed, these words? We can't know for sure. But we've included here a dozen that range widely in tone.

- John Jacob Astor IV and his wife were on the Titanic. As it began to sink he gave up his seat next to her in a lifeboat to another woman and told his wife before drowning: "The ladies have to go first. Goodbye dearie, I'll see you later."
- Humphrey Bogart, the actor who was known for heavy drinking and smoking: "I should have never switched from Scotch to Martinis."
- Dominique Bouhours, a French grammarian: "I am about to, or I am going to, die: either expression is correct."
- Winston Churchill: "I am bored with it all."
- German poet Heinrich Heine was urged to seek God's forgiveness before dying. His response: "God will forgive me; that's his job."

- Novelist W. Somerset Maugham: "Dying is a very dull, dreary affair. My advice to you is have nothing to do with it."
- Nostradamus, the sixteenth century French astrologer and reputed seer, with a prediction that proved completely accurate: "Tomorrow I shall no longer be here."
- Lawrence Oates was the Arctic explorer on Captain Scott's fateful, and failed, attempt to be the first to reach the South Pole. Suffering from frostbite and gangrene, he left the tent in what is seen as an act of self-sacrifice so that he wouldn't be a burden on his companions. He walked into a blizzard after saying: "I am just going outside and may be some time." His body was never found.
- William Palmer, a convicted poisoner, was about to step onto the scaffold when he asked, "Is it safe?"
- Lord Palmerston, former British Prime Minister: "Die, my dear doctor, that's the last thing I shall do." (Similar words are attributed to Groucho Marx.)
- Gen. John Sedgwick, a Union military man in the US Civil War, confidently looked toward enemy lines and proclaimed, "They couldn't hit an elephant at this dist...."
- Oscar Wilde, the writer and wit, was understandably accredited with more than one set of last words. One is, "This wallpaper and I are fighting a duel to the death. Either it goes or I do." And he possibly said this toward the end of his life, if not at death's door itself: "I am dying beyond my means. I can't even afford to die."

The Five Persuaders

Few people take words more seriously than copywriters in ad agencies. They are intensely aware of the power of words and choosing just the right ones can make or break a multi-million-dollar ad campaign.

We've all seen ads that we liked, perhaps because they were funny, poignant, clever or had some other quality that made them stand out. But it's no secret in the world of advertising that getting your ad noticed is only part of the challenge facing the messenger; the definition of a successful ad is that it *persuades* enough of those seeing or hearing it to justify the advertiser's expense.

How to do that? That's where word choice comes in. Research has confirmed that the following five words have the most potential for getting the results the advertiser wants.[30]

- *Because*
- *Free*
- *Instantly*
- *New*
- *You*

Each appeals to a part of our psyche in powerful ways. Try analyzing an ad or two, to see how many of these words appear—and then ask yourself how you react to those you find. How would the ad be different if those words were missing?

---

[30] https://copyblogger.com/persuasive-copywriting-words/.

Freudian Slips

A Freudian slip is a mistake word use that sets professional and amateur psychologists atwitter about the possible subconscious motivation behind the error. As the saying goes, this kind of slip is "when you say one thing and mean your mother." Named after pioneering, and highly controversial, psychologist Sigmund Freud, these mistakes can be extremely embarrassing.

The thoughtco.com website offers a delicious example from the late Sen. Edward Kennedy. In a televised speech in 1991 he said, "'Our national interest ought to be to encourage the *breast,*' he paused, then corrected himself, 'the *best* and the brightest.' The fact that his hands were suggestively cupping the air as he spoke made the moment prime for Freudian analysis."

The website also cites this slip by former President George H. W. Bush, who in a 1988 campaign speech said, "We've had triumphs. Made some mistakes. We've had some *sex...* uh... *setbacks.*"

Not all Freudian slips are explicitly linked to sex. Others may, according to one psychoanalytical theory or another, speak to someone's sublimated aggression or fear. Two possibly apocryphal stories will illustrate that point. A bishop was visiting a rural area and arrived at his hotel amidst the awe of the staff, who were greatly intimidated by this important guest. The bishop summoned the bellboy for room service and the terrified young fellow knocked on the cleric's door. "Who is it?" boomed the bishop's voice. "It's the Lord, my boy," came the reply. One could write reams of analysis, I suppose, about that response.

Story number two is about a newspaper report on a distinguished general. The copy should have described him as "this battle-scarred veteran." The typesetter (yes, this took place long ago) instead set it as "this battle-scared veteran." The general was furious and complained to the paper, which ran an apology and this correction: "We deeply regret the error. Our report should have referred to the general as 'this bottle-scarred veteran.'" What *was* going on in the typesetter's subconscious?

But do Freudian slips actually exist? Or are they merely mistakes, some of which just appear to have a sexual or otherwise significant subconscious motivation? Now, more than a century after Freud presented this idea, the relatively small number of Freudian psychologists around today would undoubtedly still affirm the reality of this concept. Many others are skeptical. A 1984 New York Times article said, "Freud read hidden meanings in every slip. But the new school of thought holds that the vast majority of slips are devoid of ulterior motives or meanings; though some may, indeed, be motivated by unconscious conflicts, more often than not, a slip is just a slip."

***

So, you ask, "What do I think of Freudian slips?" My answer: "Sorry, but I regard my choice of undergarments as a private matter."

A Gallimaufry—*noun, meaning hodgepodge*

Abracadabra—A word with supposedly magical properties, and traditionally said by magicians before they dazzle you with an illusion. Other magic words (again, supposedly) are *Alakazam* and *Hey Presto!* These are in a different category from words used in occult practices or divination, which are treated in **Prophetic Words**.

***

Bunburying—In Oscar Wilde's play, *The Importance of Being Earnest*, one of the characters invents a friend named Bunbury, a chronic invalid. He often needs to be visited at short notice and thus provides a convenient excuse to skip out of commitments. The term *bunburying* is applied to this strategy of avoiding one's commitments under false pretenses.

***

Dial—An odd choice of a word, from an earlier rotary phone era, which we keep using to describe punching numbers on a digital phone.

***

Gallimaufry—A hodgepodge (or its alternative spelling, hotchpotch). This section could be called *Miscellaneous* but why do that when the word *Gallimaufry* is available? Maybe because people are much more likely to recognize "miscellaneous"? Yes, that's a valid reason—keep it simple and easy for the reader, and all that. But this is *my* book and I want gallimaufry.[31]

***

Glass slipper—As in Cinderella. Let's hope you're seated for this one; it could be a shock if you've not yet heard this tale of a word gone wrong. The story originates with a Frenchman named Charles Perrault (1628-1703), who founded the genre of fairy tales. Among his works were *Little Red Riding Hood, Puss in Boots* and *The Sleeping Beauty*. And, of course, *Cinderella*. The original title of Cinderella was *La Petite Pantoufle de Vair*, or *The Little Fur Slipper*. However, somewhere along the line the sound of "vair" got confused with "verre," which means glass, and we've misconstrued a critical part of Perrault's story ever since.

***

Happiness—I will never be able to look at this word quite the same way since reading the anecdote about Mrs. De Gaulle, wife of the great French statesman and president, General Charles De Gaulle. Upon his retirement the De Gaulles were having lunch with some English friends. She was asked what she was most looking forward to in this new chapter. She replied: "A penis." The general then said, "My dear, I think the English don't pronounce the word quite like that. It's *'appiness.*"[32]

***

---

[31] Author moves into corner and sits on floor, adopting a level-three moue.
"What's a 'moue'?"
It's a pout.
"Why not just say 'pout'?"
'Cause it's *my* book and I want to say "*moue.*" [Moves farther into corner....]
[32] Cited in Clifton Fadiman, ed, *The Little Brown Book of Anecdotes.*

MacGuffin—This word, popularized by the movie director Alfred Hitchcock, refers to a plot device in a film that helps drive the narrative forward but isn't of intrinsic value to the story. An example is in his film *Vertigo*, where a spare apartment key plays this role. In the thriller *Ronin*, a group of mercenaries try to steal a briefcase for the IRA, which is also sought by the Russian mafia. You never learn what's in the briefcase but it's what drives the entire movie.

***

Oogly-boogly—Something scary that jumps out at you in a horror movie.

***

Pease—As in the nursery rhyme, "pease porridge hot, pease porridge cold." This word, which is now largely obsolete, was thought to be a plural of *pea* and as a result was "back-formed" (that's the technical term), to become the legume we know and love today as a *pea*.

***

Swell and *Lousy*—"I know only two words of American slang, *swell* and *lousy*. I think *swell* is lousy, but *lousy* is swell."
—J.B. Priestley, British novelist and playwright

***

Two Witty Theatre Reviews—Because there's no other logical place in the book for these, I am including here two brief, and now classic, theatre reviews. A play titled *I Am a Camera* drew the response, "No Leica" from New York critic Walter Kerr. And the review of the production *Yes!* was even shorter: "No!"

***

Yahweh—To the Old Testament Hebrews, the name of God was so holy that it couldn't be said aloud or even spelled out in full. Usually represented by the letters YHWH, it is usually referred to in contemporary Bibles as the "LORD," in capital letters.

German Words

Life is too short to learn German.
  —Richard Porson

***

German is only one of dozens of languages from which English has siphoned off whatever words it thinks it can use. Fortunately it's only these borrowed words that English speakers need to use; we don't need to incorporate what for English-speakers is the complex grammar of contemporary German.

But first, a joke poking fun at one aspect of German grammar that can frustrate English speakers. An English-speaking businessman, with his translator, is meeting with his German counterpart. The initial greetings go well but a few minutes into the conversation the German keeps talking, and talking, and talking. Eventually the English-speaker whispers to the translator, "What's he saying?" And the translator replies, "Please, I'm waiting for the verb."

1. *Bildungsroman*—A novel about the moral and psychological growth of the main character.
2. *Drachenfutter*—Literally "dragon fodder," the word is used to refer to a gift of candy or flowers to placate an angry wife (presumably after the gift-bearer has done something deserving of her anger).
3. *Luftmensch*—An impractical contemplative person having no definite business or income.
4. *Materialschlacht*—A battle of hardware.

5. *Schadenfreude*—The pleasure you feel at someone else's misfortune.

6. *Schlagfertig*—"Ready with a hit," as in a quick response in repartee.

7. *Sitzfleisch*—The ability to sit through or tolerate something boring; the ability to endure or persist in a task.

8. *Sitzkrieg*—A period of war marked by little or no active hostilities.

9. *Sturm und drang*—Storm and stress, or turmoil.

10. *Weltschmerz*—Depression or apathy caused by what one sees as the state of the world.

11. *Witzelsucht*—A pathological compulsion to tell jokes, puns, and laugh uproariously at one's own humor; a medical condition with a brain abnormality.

12. *Zeitgeber*—An environmental cue, such as light, that helps to regulate the biological clock of an organism.

Goldwynisms

Sam Goldwyn became a titan as a Hollywood producer, overcoming his humble beginnings as a young Polish immigrant. But that's only one way he secured his place in history. Another is a series of odd sentences, filled with illogical or somehow broken syntax. Some of these sayings were indeed his own. But more than any other celebrity in recent times, he was credited with far more entertaining sayings than he actually said.

For example, one of the movie giants of his time was Orson Welles, whom he kept pursuing to make a movie for him. Welles kept refusing. Then, on one occasion, according to Paul F. Boller and John George, "he backed Welles into a corner and argued so forcibly that the great film-maker seemed to be yielding. Finally Goldwyn cried: 'Look, Orson, if you'll just say yes to doing a picture with me, I'll give you a blank check right now.'"[33]

But a gossip columnist wrote that Goldwyn had said, "I'll give you a *blanket* check"—the kind of mangled speech people associated with the movie giant. Boller and George note that the report angered Goldwyn, adding: "He was even angrier when the *Reader's Digest* printed the "blanket-check" quote in its 'Picturesque Patter of Speech' column and sent him a check for $25."

And so it went for Goldwyn. He forever became known for these distinctive sayings, to the point that "Goldwynism" is a recognized word. Merriam-Webster defines it as "a phrase or

---

[33] Paul F. Boller Jr. and John George, *They Never Said It: A Book of Fake Quotes, Misquotes and Misleading Attributions*, 37.

expression (as 'include me out') involving a grotesque use of a word."

Alas, enjoyable though these supposed quotes are, Boller and George are among many writers who point out that few of these sayings attributed to Goldwyn are genuine. Many were written by the public relations people at Metro-Goldwyn-Mayer, to exploit the attention they garnered. Others were generated by writers like George Oppenheimer, a theatre critic for *Newsday*. He, together with writers like Dorothy Parker and Edna Ferber, would place bets on who could make up the best Goldwyn-sounding statements. On one occasion he won with a supposed Goldwyn response to criticism: "'It rolls off my back like a duck' was one of mine,"[34] Oppenheimer said.

So, on the understanding that the Goldwynisms listed here are of dubious authenticity, I have included them for the sheer enjoyment they provide.

- A verbal agreement isn't worth the paper it's written on.
- Anyone who goes to a psychiatrist ought to have his head examined.
- Destroy all this correspondence, it's cluttering up the office—but be sure to keep a copy of every letter.
- He isn't as big a dope as I give him credit for.
- I can answer you in two words: im possible.
- I feel lousy. I must've woke up on the wrong side of the street.

---

[34] Boller and George, 39.

Harsh Words

Maybe your Mom told you that if you didn't have anything nice to say about someone, don't say anything at all. C'mon—what sort of self-deluding idiot is going follow that dumb advice?

OK. Just warming up here, trying to get into the spirit of things. With so much nastiness and vituperative flooding our social media and public discourse these days, we'd certainly serve the common good by heeding Mom's advice. Still, this is a book about words. And some crafters of insults have employed words to masterful effect as they rounded on their targets; we want to recognize that cleverness with words.

However, let's first deal with an unfortunate reality: Many famous insults are of dubious authenticity. Most of us are familiar with some of Winston Churchill's barbs. One of the best known is the exchange between him and Lady Astor, who said, "If I were your wife, I'd put poison in your tea." And his reply, "And if I were your husband, I'd drink it."

Another story is that he was drunk and a woman politician (who, exactly, varies with the telling) told Churchill, "You are disgustingly drunk." He replied, "And you are ugly. But tomorrow I shall be sober."

Unfortunately, both these quotations associated with Churchill have been debunked by the quoteinvestigator.com website. The site documents how multiple versions of these retorts go way back, as far as 1863 for the "I shall be sober" line. An almost identical exchange on the poison quip was first reported in a New York newspaper in 1899. The site concludes that the prime minister had most likely heard these stories and adapted them for the occasion—that is, if he said them at all.

One that is apparently authenticated was reported by his secretary. [Warning: Crudity ahead.] He told Churchill while he was on the toilet that a senior government official was on the phone and wanted to talk to him. Churchill said, "Tell him I can deal with only one sh*t at a time."

***

Now let's look at what I call Olympics-level insults, those of such verbal dexterity and/or imagination that they would merit advancing to the medal round of the World Insult Olympiad, if there were such a thing.

Anybody can say rude things about someone. If I say, "Abigail is a fool," you may be shocked I said that about her. But there's nothing original or imaginative about my insult. Instead, an Olympics qualifier will take you by surprise and is most likely an insult you will remember far more for what was said than its target. Another test is that you'd want to store the insult in your memory and, Churchill-like, use it as if it were your own creation if you get the opportunity.

The Olympic Committee has three rules: (1) There's only one entry per contestant, so a wit like Dorothy Parker or Oscar Wilde can put forward only his or her best offering; (2) the target of the insult must be specified; and (3) the entry is not to be confused with **Repartee**, which is a possibly insulting comment but one triggered by the other party. The Committee regards a true insult as one initiated by the insulter.

Here then are ten entries. You get to speculate on who might take the gold and who else might medal.

- James Dickey on fellow poet Robert Frost: "If it were thought anything I wrote was influenced by Robert Frost, I would take that particular work of mine, shred it, and flush it down the toilet, hoping not to clog the pipes. A more sententious, holding-forth old bore who expected every hero-worshipping adenoidal little twerp of a student-poet to hang on his every word I never saw."

- British Prime Minister Benjamin Disraeli, on Lord Russell: "If a traveler were informed that such a man was leader of the House of Commons, he may well begin to comprehend how the Egyptians worshipped a stick insect."

- British Prime Minister David Lloyd George on fellow politician Herbert Samuel: "When they circumcised Herbert Samuel they threw away the wrong bit."

- Director John Huston on actor Peter O'Toole: "He looks like he's walking around just to save funeral expenses."

- Critic Clive James on tennis player John McEnroe: "As charming as a dead mouse in a loaf of bread."

- Writer Florence King about columnist Molly Ivins: "[She] delivers laid-back wisdom with the serenity of a down-home Buddha who has discovered that stool softeners really work."

- Writer Dorothy Parker on actress Dame Edith Evans: "To me, she looks like something that would eat its young."

- Journalist Edward Pearce on British Prime Minister John Major: "The only man who ran away from the circus to become an accountant."

- Journalist James Reston on Richard Nixon: "He inherited some good instincts from his Quaker forebears but by diligent hard work he overcame them."

- Oscar Wilde, on playwright Henry Arthur Jones: "The first rule for a young playwright to follow is not to write like Henry Arthur Jones. The second and third rules are the same."

***

Insults need not be limited to people. The French statesman George Clemenceau said the United States was "the only nation in history that has gone from barbarism to decadence without passing through the intervening stage of civilization."

What of America's northern neighbor? Canadian author John Colombo famously said of his own country that "Canada could have enjoyed English government, French culture, and American know-how. Instead it ended up with English know-how, French government, and American culture."

Literature and popular culture bring us their contributions too. One of my favorites is from H. H. Munro, better known by his pen name "Saki." He was a gifted satirist whose witty short stories are sadly now hardly known in the English-speaking world. His life was cut short when he was killed in France in World War I. One of his most memorable lines was: "He is one of those people who would be enormously improved by death."

Pop culture has given us the often hilarious series of "Your Momma" jokes ("Your Momma's so fat it takes an hour's drive to get on her good side" and "Your Momma's so fat she has her own ZIP code.") We are now veering into sensitive territory. Some may find Momma's size to be nothing to laugh at, or that the other examples here are steeped in a wide range of cruelties. Well, let me steer you instead to **Kind Words**. Maybe that will help. The rest of you may want to look at **Political Correctness**.

Headlines

When the underdog Caledonian Thistles took on Celtic in a 2000 Scottish Cup soccer match, they unexpectedly won: 3-1. But two decades later, what's remembered as much as, or even more than, the match itself was the headline the *Sun* newspaper used to announce the Caledonian (or "Caley") victory: *Super Caley Go Ballistic, Celtic Are Atrocious.* (You need to say this aloud and if you still don't get it, think "Mary Poppins.")

That is an ingeniously inventive headline, telling the story with flair and a superb use of words. But it's far from the only one from the creative minds of copy editors around the world. Others from the world of sports include this one on a story about timekeepers who note athletes' times during training: "These are the souls that time men's tries"—a play on Thomas Paine's memorable words, "These are the times that try men's souls."

The Wimbledon tennis tournament provided fodder for another ingenious headline, with a double pun. The 1987 men's final was between the Australian Pat Cash and a Czech, Ivan Lendl. At least one paper headlined the upcoming match by asking, "Will it be Cash or a Czech?" Cash won.

Another play on words had to do with the capital of Albania. *The Guardian* newspaper ran a story from the capital city, Tirana, about the economic revival in that country, with this headline: "Tirana Boom Today" (relying on the 1942 song "Ta-ra-ra-boom-de-ay").

***

Headlines are usually far more prosaic than these examples. But each headline has to accomplish the same task: tell the story accurately and in a handful of words, either to draw the reader in or give the reader permission to skip the story altogether. Complex stories can present a significant challenge to the headline writer. Take for example the circumstances that led to a celebrated headline in New York's *Daily News*. The city was in serious financial trouble in the 1970s and sought help from the federal government and then-president Gerald Ford. He said he'd veto any request that Congress approved. How to capture all of this in just a few words? The paper came up with: "Ford to City: Drop Dead."

Other headlines have jumped the gun (or at least, their writers have) on big stories. Like the Brazilian paper, *O Mundo*, which proclaimed in advance their country's victory in the World Cup soccer final in 1950—but didn't take into account Uruguay's 2-1 victory later that day.

Given the time constraints facing newspapers and the need to go to print while a story is still unfolding, editors will occasionally take a chance. That risk-taking didn't work well for *The Chicago Daily Tribune* (now just *The Chicago Tribune*) on Nov. 3, 1948, when it incorrectly and infamously proclaimed Thomas Dewey as beating incumbent Harry Truman in the presidential race. The iconic photo of a beaming Truman holding aloft a copy of the paper, with its wrong headline, remains an object lesson to hasty editors everywhere.

Imagined Proverbs

The *New Statesman* magazine has long hosted ingenious competitions in which readers submit parodies, satires, or other humorous responses to a weekly challenge. Now and again they're invited to submit made up but nevertheless wise-sounding proverbs. Try memorizing a few and, when the moment is right, slip one into conversation, as if everyone's expected to know it. Here's a sampling.

1. A hungry camel sinks less deeply into the sand.
2. An owl in a sack troubles no man.
3. One man's meat is rarely enough for two.
4. Little pitchers hold little water.
5. The pen is cheaper than the laptop.
6. You won't find milk in a whisky bottle.
7. No wooden ball bounces high.
8. Small change buys only small things.
9. Every book has a first page.
10. Many a bad joke is spoken in jest.
11. There's none so deaf as those who cannot hear.
12. Ringtones don't select themselves.
13. Black yaks pay no tax.
14. Umbrellas do not pray for rain.
15. Age will come to those who wait.

A Joke About Words

Once there were two young brothers. The five-year-old announced it was time for them to start using bad words. Of course, his four-year-old brother agreed. The next morning Mom asked the boys what they wanted for breakfast. Seizing the moment, the older boy said, "Oh, what the hell, I'll have Wheaties." Horrified, the Mom spanked the boy, gave him a furious lecture on acceptable words in their family, and sent him to his room hungry.

She then turned to the younger boy, sitting terrified as he watched what had happened. "And you?" she demanded. He replied, "Well, I'm not sure, but you can bet your ass it won't be Wheaties."

Kind Words

To use bitter words, when kind words are at hand, is like picking unripe fruit when the ripe fruit is there.
—Thiruvalluvar

One kind word can warm three winter months.
—Japanese proverb

Anna Lappé, an American writer, said "Every time you spend money, you're casting a vote for the kind of world you want." It's not too much of a stretch to say that you're doing the same with the words or sentences you speak or write for others to read. Whether we know it or not, we are influencing people all the time. Perhaps it's the woman at the customer service counter at Walmart, our young preschooler, our boss, or that insecure new hire you're supervising and who is unsure how well he's doing.

This category consists of the words it was well to leave unspoken and the ones of encouragement that were. There's not much to say here, as the need not to say unkind things and to say kind ones instead is self-evident. But as we noted in **Harsh Words**, we live in an era when angry and even hateful speech characterizes much of our politics, our grievances, and our portrayals of our opponents. Much of our animosity is protected by the shield of anonymity that social media afford us and so we feel free to let rip.

What choice will we make, at the end of a crappy day, when we need to correct our child for the umpteenth time? Or how will we speak with that beleaguered customer service woman at Walmart? Even though you're irritated at needing to return a pair of pants that split the first time you wore them, is that *her* fault? Probably the dozens of other customers who've spoken to her today have conveyed the sense that she's personally to blame for their problem—if not in actual words, at least in their tone.

Maybe you can offer her three things: a kind word of greeting accompanied by a smile and thanking her for being available to help you; another thank you for her help; and then a bonus she's not expecting: something like "I appreciate your important work in this store; I really am grateful for your help today." No, this isn't a plea for saccharine mushiness. Rather, it's an encouragement to play your infinitely small part in advancing civilization itself. As English novelist Louis de Bernieres said, "The real index of civilization is when people are kinder than they need to be."

See also **Tact**.

The KISS Rule

The rule is, *Keep It Simple, Stupid.* Illustrative mini-drama to follow.

The Setting: Washington DC, during World War II.

The Players: An unidentified government official charged with safety; the President of the United States, Franklin Roosevelt.

Unidentified Official: Steps on stage with this proclamation.

Such preparations shall be made as will completely obscure all Federal buildings and non-Federal buildings occupied by the Federal government for any period of time from visibility by internal or external illumination. Such obscuration may be obtained either by: blackout construction or by termination of the illumination.

President Roosevelt: He has somehow found out about this proclamation and rewritten it.

Tell them that in buildings where they have to keep the work going, to put something over the windows, and in buildings where they can let the work stop for a while, to turn out the lights.

Unidentified Official: Hangs head in shame, skulks off stage left.

***

Now, a test: Read the sentence that follows and decide immediately if you want to see the show: *"This is a show which you must not fail to miss."*

So, what is it: Do you want to see this show? Yes? No? Have no idea? One can work through the positives and negatives like a logician and come up with a technically correct answer. But you'll still be in the dark on what this theatre critic meant.

Let's look at three more examples. The first is also from the world of government. It's somewhat dated, as the numbers indicate, but it's worth sharing here. This is an excerpt from a letter this agency sent out to more than 100,000 people over a period of seven years: "In order to be fully insured, an individual must have earned $50 or more in covered employment for as many quarters of coverage as half the calendar quarters elapsing between 1935 and the quarter in which he reaches 65 or dies, whichever first occurs."

The second is more recent. It concerns a vote in Colorado on a proposed constitutional amendment: "Shall there be an amendment to the Colorado constitution concerning the removal of the exception to the prohibition of slavery and involuntary servitude when used as a punishment for person duly convicted of a crime." Yes, well....

Finally, there's this: "It is incumbent upon us to utilize and leverage our core competencies to maximize our traction in the verticals." Apparently, this translates into, "We should focus on what we do well."

Each of these writers forgot about the KISS rule. They failed to ask, "What *exactly* do I want to say? OK, now say it." They also forgot the "Mom Test." I'd tell a student that while I had never met his or her Mom, I assumed she was a sharp woman. "Would she immediately understand what you've written?" I would ask. If not, what can you do to fix what you've written? Pity that the writers of the examples cited here never ran them by Mom.

Latin Legacy

English is shaped to a massive degree by Latin. Increasingly, other languages find their vocabularies are also being raided by English and pulled into its orbit. It is as if this world language were some linguistic black hole, too powerful for any other language to resist, as we saw in **Borrowed Words**. But Latin remains foundational to English; all those early inclusions into English form the core of this black hole.

Here are a dozen common expressions.

1. *Ad hoc*—For a particular purpose.
2. *Ad infinitum*—Without end.
3. *Bona fide*—Made in good faith.
4. *Caveat emptor*—Let the buyer beware.
5. *Circa*—About, usually referring to dates.
6. *De facto*—Actually so, in reality.
7. *Et alia*[35]—And others, usually written as *et al.*
8. *In absentia*—In absence.
9. *Modus operandi*—Method of operation.
10. *Non sequitur*—A statement that doesn't logically follow what preceded it (see entry on **Non Sequitur**).
11. *Nota bene*—Note well, usually written as *N.B.*
12. *Pro bono publico*—For the public good.

But this is just scratching the surface. Let's move on to another category of Latin expressions, which tell us even more....

---

[35] "That's no relation to *Al Italia*, is it?"
"No, you're thinking of the Italian airline."

Latin Mottos, Wisdom *et al*

The high school I attended in Cape Town had a motto, as was typical of many British and South African institutions. And for it to be a proper motto, it had to be in Latin. Ours was: *Laborare est orare.* That translates as "to work is to pray." Many of us understood it to mean "to work is to play," which didn't make much sense. Come to think of it, "to work is to pray" didn't make much sense to us 12- to 17-year-old boys either.

Below are some other Latin mottos or phrases I have encountered over the years and which I thought worth recording. Maybe you'll want to announce to your children over dinner tonight that henceforth your family motto will be *Aliis licet: tibi non licet.* That would have made much more sense to us high schoolers than *laborare est orare.*

***

- *Aliis licet: tibi non licet*—Others may, you may not.
- *Capax dei*—A capacity for God.
- *Cavendo tutus*—Safely through caution. This is the motto of the Dukes of Devonshire, members of the Cavendish family.
- *Festina lente*—A delicious oxymoron, meaning hasten slowly.
- *Ignotum per ignotius*—The unknown by the even less known, used of an explanation that is more confusing than what it is meant to explain.
- *Ingratum si dixeris, omnia dicis*—If you pronounce a man ungrateful, you say all that can be said against him.

- *Invenimus et delimus*—The motto of an anti-shipping squadron of the Royal Australian Air Force, meaning "we find and destroy."
- *Memento mori*—Be mindful of dying; that is, do not forget that you are only human.
- *Quis custodiet ipsos custodes?*—Who will guard the guardians? Or, Who will watch the watchers?
- *Ultima thule*—A place beyond the borders of the known world.

Lay and Lie

My wife and I volunteer at a crisis nursery in our community, an invaluable resource for Moms and Dads who urgently need respite help in taking care of their kids—or who have no babysitter available while Mom goes for a job interview or to a doctor's appointment. Whatever the need, the nursery is available at no charge for parents needing help, twenty-four hours a day, every day of the year. The kids typically range in age from babies up to age 6.

As our three-hour shift draws to an end and bedtime approaches, we help the professional staff ready the kids for bed. Of course, not all of them like that idea. Some persist in sitting up, talking, or getting out of bed. That's when one of the staff is likely to tell a child, "Now, lay down."

Whether the child responds or not, I do—silently. I clench my teeth. Here they are, vulnerable and highly malleable toddlers and preschoolers, being schooled in wayward English usage from their earliest days. I sigh. Then I concede that if they're not going to be led astray tonight, it will happen later, prompted by other unwitting souls who don't know the difference between *lay* and *lie*. Nothing I can do will stop this. But *you*? The fact that you've read this far indicates that you care. Thank you, thank you. So here goes:

The Great "Lie" and "Lay" Confusion Resolved Once and for All

Step 1 is to know there are two words quite distinct in meaning. Which one do you want: *Lay* or *Lie*?

Lay means "to put in place"—it always takes an object.

The chicken lays an egg. I lay the table.

Lie means "to recline"—it never takes an object.
(Don't confuse with "Don't lie to me, you hypocrite.")

Now for <u>Step 2</u>: The hard part—can you fill in the blanks?

	Present Participle *I am now*	Past Tense *Yesterday I*	Past Participle *Before you called, I had*
Lay an egg	_____-ing an egg	___ an egg	___ an egg
Lie down	___ ing down	___down	___ down

Now for <u>Step 2A:</u> The hard part resolved.

	Present Participle *I am now*	Past Tense *Yesterday I*	Past Participle *Before you called, I had*
Lay an egg	laying an egg	Laid an egg	laid an egg
Lie down	lying down	Lay down	lain down

Libelous Words

You know the rhyme your Mom may have taught you after the kid next door called you nasty names:

Sticks and stones may break my bones
But words will never hurt me.

Mom had good intentions but probably hadn't taken a course in media law. If she had, she may have taught you a more accurate version:

Sticks and stones may break my bones
But words will never hurt me.
But that's just not so, because:
Of all those nasty libel laws.

Admittedly, even in this litigious society we don't hear of 7-year-olds confronting each other in court in a bitterly contested libel suit. With grown-ups, it's a different matter. It certainly could have ended up that way in my hometown of Spokane in November 2000. An intern working on the copy desk at the local paper, *The Spokesman-Review*, was a disgruntled young woman. She was a graduate of Gonzaga University, the local Jesuit institution. Its president, Fr. Robert Spitzer, had earlier in the year banned a Planned Parenthood representative from speaking on campus, a stand this intern strongly opposed.

The intern, who was laying out pages, came across a brief story about an upcoming talk Fr. Spitzer was to give on his new book. She then inserted a "space-holder" headline on the story. That in itself wasn't a problem; copy editors do that often, even though they know the risk that they might forget to insert the actual headline later. (You've probably seen headlines reading something like "Head to come.")

The problem was the headline she chose: "Nazi Priest Promotes His Book." And yes, you've correctly guessed what happened. Somehow, in the rush of finishing up the paper nobody replaced the headline and thousands of readers in the Spokane area got word the next morning that the Gonzaga University president was a Nazi.

As I told my media law students after showing them the headline, Fr. Spitzer could have shown up at the newspaper's offices on Riverside Avenue with a wheelbarrow and said: "Please fill it up with money." This was such an open-and-shut case of libel that the paper's lawyer had to be stupendously grateful that the man they had libeled knew something about forgiveness. Following groveling apologies from the paper (and the firing of the intern), life in sleepy Spokane settled down to normal once again.

***

All this is to say that words can get you into serious trouble. Libeling someone means you've said something about a person that would damage his or her reputation or character, or cause people to avoid that person. So, if I wrote that you were a cheat or frequented prostitutes or had genital herpes, you could argue in court that my words had hurt you. Of course, my lawyer would try to argue that what I said was true.

US libel law allows media organizations considerable leeway in making genuine mistakes if they libel public figures—that is, people like politicians and celebrities. They have a tough time winning a libel suit. For ordinary people, like you and me, the standards are different if we think we've been wronged and want to sue. It's easier, but still not easy, for us to win a case.

But our focus here is on what we could call "red-flag" words, which could get you in trouble in court. Calling someone a liar, thief, embezzler would harm that person's reputation. Similarly, if you wrote that Dr. Dennis Dentist was a butcher who shouldn't be allowed near patients, you could expect trouble. And if you said someone had leprosy or AIDS, which could cause others to avoid that person, once more you'd be in hot water. Sometimes a libelous statement is situational. Stating that someone is an atheist isn't necessarily libelous. But if you wrote that about someone whom your church leadership was considering as the church's next pastor, that would be a different matter.

The news media libel people every day. They do so, however, well aware of the tested protections or defenses they can call upon if they are sued. For example, if my local paper says I stole money from my employer, and it's true, I can't win a libel suit. What if the paper runs a story about my trial for embezzlement and reports all sort of allegations that surface that make me look bad, but then I am acquitted? If the paper has fairly reported all those nasty things that were said about me in court, I can't sue. Because it happened in a courtroom, the paper has what is known as a defense of privilege. Similar protections are given the media for reporting what could be libelous statements made in a city council meeting or the state legislature, for example.

Occasionally though media slip up and find themselves losing a libel judgment. It's not only media organizations that can be sued. In 2019 Oberlin College in Ohio was ordered to pay $44.4 million in damages to a local business, which a jury found the college had libeled. That's a whole lot of wheelbarrows full of cash.

Most ordinary people don't get sued for libel because lawyers know that individuals typically don't have enough money to make it worth their while, either for the client who believes he or she has been wronged, or for the contingency fee the lawyer hopes to secure. Still, these days we need to be especially attentive what we may write about someone on social media.

If your only take-away from this book is the need for caution when saying nasty things about other people, then you may have got your money's worth multiple times over.

Long Words

Alice had not the slightest idea what latitude was, or longitude either, but she thought they were nice grand words to say.
— Lewis Carroll

A major problem here is, what do we mean by "word"? Are we talking about everyday words? Words that get used on special occasions, or are part of specialist (typically scientific) vocabularies? Or made-up words? Think of the one Mary Poppins brought to life:

- *Supercalifragilisticexpialidocious* (34 letters)

The lexico.com website offers three words for our consideration:

- *Antidisestablishmentarianism* (28 letters), meaning "opposition to the disestablishment of the Church of England."
- *Floccinaucinihilipilification* (29 letters), meaning "the estimation of something as worthless."
- *Pneumonoultramicroscopicsilicovolcanoconiosis* (45 letters), meaning "a lung disease."

To be realistic, though, when did you last hear any of these in conversation? Nor are you likely to hear this next one, all the more because it's the ultimate conversation killer: It takes an estimated three and a half hours to say, running as it does to

189,819 letters. It's the name of a giant protein called titin. Can we seriously regard a construction this long as a genuine word? Surely not. But in case there's some smart aleck out there who would otherwise find fault if we did not refer to this contender, we are including it here for completeness' sake.

Ten Words Beginning with M

This is an unexpected entry, resulting from a mediated agreement between the author's legal representative and the trade union representing the letter M. The union argued that their members were unfairly treated because **Mumpsimus** was singled out for special recognition and received an entry of its own. The union initially demanded that fifty other words beginning with M be accorded special recognition in this volume. Following mediation it was agreed that ten words (of the author's choosing) would be included, and that the author would ask the publisher to record the copyright date of the book in Roman letters—MMXXI for 2021, to provide a deservedly wider recognition of this noble letter.

1. *Maffick*—Rejoice or celebrate with boisterous public demonstrations, from the lifting of the 217-day siege of Mafeking in South Africa, during the Boer War.
2. *Mahout*—A keeper and driver of an elephant.
3. *Malism*—The belief that the world is evil.
4. *Manqué*—Having had ambition or potential but without it being fulfilled; for example, "a poet manqué."
5. *Marabout*—A Muslim hermit.
6. *Megillah*—Any long, boring story.
7. *Minyan*—The minimum number of people required by Jewish law to be present for a religious service to be held, that is, ten adult males.
8. *Misodoctakleidist*—One who hates to practice the piano.
9. *Moue*—A grimace of discontent, a pout.
10. *Mufti*—Plain clothes worn by someone usually wearing a uniform.

Malapropisms

Meet Mrs. Malaprop, one of the most endearing characters in English literature. She entered the world in Richard Brinsley Sheridan's play, *The Rivals*, in 1775. Her distinguishing feature is her repeated use of the wrong, but similar sounding, word to express herself—with amusing results. For instance, she says "*illiterate* him quite from your memory," "he is the very *pineapple* of politeness," and "she's as headstrong as an *allegory* on the banks of the Nile" (instead of *obliterate*, *pinnacle* and *alligator*).

And in one jam-packed sentence, Sheridan has her say, "Sure, if I *reprehend* anything in this world it is the use of my *oracular* tongue, and a nice *derangement* of *epitaphs*" (instead of *apprehend*, *vernacular, arrangement*, and *epithets*). His audiences would have roared with laughter.

Sheridan wasn't first the first to employ this device, however. Shakespeare used it, especially with his character Dogberry in *Much Ado About Nothing*. Many other writers have used it since. The most amusing unintentional examples come from politicians, who—for some odd reason—we expect to know better when using the English language in public. So we have from three former politicians:

- Texas Governor Rick Perry described states as "*lavatories* of innovation and democracy" (instead of *laboratories*).
- Chicago Mayor Richard J. Daley referred to "Alcoholics *Unanimous* (instead of *Anonymous*).
- Vice President Dan Quayle assured us that "Republicans understand the importance of *bondage*

between a mother and child." (If you need an explanation for this one, you're in need of more help than this book can provide.)

***

Sheridan presumably named this character based on the word *malapropos*, meaning "inappropriate" or "inappropriately." And speaking of appropriateness, the *New Scientist* magazine reported that an office worker had described a colleague as "a vast *suppository* of information." Recognizing his error, he then apologized for his "*Miss-Marple-ism*," which the magazine said was possibly the first time anyone had uttered a malapropism for the word malapropism itself.

See also **Mixed Metaphors** and **Mondegreens**, each of which also offers much merriment.

The Meaning of Liff

Douglas Adams is best known for *The Hitchhiker's Guide to the Galaxy*, a comic science fiction concept that grew out of a BBC radio show into a best-selling book. The material was also adapted into a stage show and a film.

But it's another of his works on which we will focus here. In 1983 he and co-author John Lloyd published *The Meaning of Liff*, an inventive list of "definitions" of words—almost all of them British and Irish place names. For example, an early entry is *Alltami*, a small village in Wales, which Adams and Lloyd define as "The ancient art of being able to balance the hot and cold shower taps."

Then there's *Hickling*, another village, in Norfolk, which according to Adams and Lloyd, is "The practice of infuriating theatre-goers by not only arriving late to a center-row seat, but also loudly apologizing to and patting each member of the audience in turn."

Most of the place names that they use as triggers for their wild creativity are similarly obscure. A few more examples:

- *Babsworth*—Something which justifies having a really good cry.
- *Cromarty*—The brittle sludge which clings to the top of ketchup bottles and plastic tomatoes in nasty cafes.
- *Dewlish*—Of the hands and feet. Prunelike after an overlong bath.
- *Ely*—The first, tiniest inkling you get that something, somewhere, has gone terribly wrong.

***

Not all the places are obscure, though. For instance, they include *Margate*, a seaside resort on the southern English coast, which they define as "a particular kind of commissionaire who sees you every day and is on cheerful Christian-name terms with you, then one day refuses to let you in because you've forgotten your identity card."

It's a book that provides recurring amusement because you can't possibly recall all the definitions. So when you re-read it, many of them seem like first encounters.

***

Not to detract from Adams and Lloyd's creativity, it's important to note that their idea was not original. Paul Jennings was a columnist for *The Observer* newspaper in London, who had in the 1960s written a piece titled "Ware, Wye, Watford," which was a more cerebral and refined forerunner of the sometimes bawdy entries in *The Meaning of Liff*.

Noting that Adam in the Bible was charged with naming all the creatures, Jennings says that British place names "not only describe places. They carry wonderful overtones, they seem to have been drawn from some huge, carelessly profuse stock of primal meaning, to have come out of the very bag from which Adam got his names." He goes on to "illustrate with a few examples from this vast English treasury of subconscious meaning...." Herewith three examples.[36]

- *Barnstaple.* Noun. Mainstay, keystone. "Mrs. Thomas is the barnstaple of our committee."
- *Ilkley.* Adjective. Having large elbows.

---

[36] Jennings' column appears in an anthology titled *The Jenguin Pennings,* published, not surprisingly, by Penguin.

- *Wembley.* Adjective. Suffering from a vague malaise. "I feel a bit wembley this morning."

***

Back to the book by Adams and Lloyd. If you're still waiting for the definition of the title word, *Liff,*[37] thank you for your patience; we haven't forgotten. Here it is: "A book, the contents of which are totally belied by its cover. For instance, any book the dust jacket of which bears the words 'This book will change your life.'"[38]

---

[37] A village in Scotland, near Dundee.
[38] Adams and Lloyd published a follow-up volume, *The Deeper Meaning of Liff,* in 1990.

Meaningless Words

While these words of course have a meaning (your dictionary will confirm that), in fact they actually serve as fillers. By the way, they are basically common in spoken English, which may be peppered with frequent uses of *like* or *really* or *you know* to keep that sentence moving.

Let's try that again: While these words ~~of course~~ have a meaning (your dictionary will confirm that), ~~in fact~~ they ~~actually~~ serve as fillers. ~~By the way~~ They are ~~basically~~ common in spoken English....

This isn't a new phenomenon. *A Dictionary of Modern English Usage,*[39] by Fowler and Gowers, which isn't all that modern anymore, spoke accurately to this point nearly a century ago. An entry on "Meaningless Words" reads:

Words and phrases are often used in a conversation, especially by the young, not as significant terms but rather, so far as they have any purpose at all, as aids of the same kind as are given in writing by punctuation, inverted commas, and underlining. It is a phenomenon perhaps more suitable for the psychologist than for the philologist. Words and phrases so employed change frequently, for they are soon worn out by overwork. Between the wars the most popular were definitely and sort of thing.... But any meaning they ever had was soon rubbed off them, and they became noises

---

[39] This work by H. W. Fowler first appeared in 1926 and a second edition, revised by Sir Ernest Gowers, was published four decades later. Fowler and Gowers were scholars to whom decades of English speakers turned for guidance on usage.

automatically produced. Their immediate successors have been actually...and you know.

***

Despite their contention that these meaningless words change frequently, the examples they cite of *actually* and *you know* are with us still. Fowler and Gowers say regarding *you know* that "it seems a compendious way of saying 'I know I am expressing myself badly, but I am sure you are intelligent enough to grasp my meaning.'"

Another meaningless word is *well*, as in "Well, I suppose we should be going." To get things in perspective, these are not evil words. But used to excess they mark someone's speech as lacking confidence or steeped in laziness, or even a lack of engagement in the conversation. Whatever.

- *Actually*
- *Basically*
- *By the way*
- *Definitely*
- *In fact*
- *Like*
- *Of course*
- *Sort of thing*
- *Really*
- *Very*
- *Well*
- *Whatever*
- *You know*

Spike Milligan

Most Americans are familiar with Monty Python and that troupe's distinctive, sometimes surreal, humor. But few people this side of the Atlantic are familiar with Spike Milligan. That's a pity, as Irish-born Milligan was a comic genius whose facility with words made him a legend in British comedy. He was best known for his work in the 1950s on a BBC radio program called *The Goon Show*, a half-hour show relying on absurd plots, word-play, sound effects, and the uncanny gift of mimicry by another brilliant comic: a young Peter Sellers. Later famous for his role in dozens of movies, like the Pink Panther series as well as more serious films like *Being There*, Sellers saw his career take off with this show. The third member of the cast was a fellow named Harry Secombe.

But it was Milligan whose wordplay and surreal thinking established him as an icon in British comedy, and whose break-the-mold humor was a precursor to the Monty Python shows. What Monty Python was to TV, Milligan was to radio.

Milligan was also well known for his books, including autobiographical accounts of his experience in World War II, such as *Adolf Hitler: My Part in His Downfall*. During much of his career he suffered from mental illness; he was manic depressive and wrote of the torment he experienced during the worst seasons of his life. It was his humor, however, for which people remember him—especially those, like me, who grew up in Britain or other English-speaking countries, listening to the original *Goon Show* broadcasts or its reruns.

In a tribute to a man who brought laughter to countless listeners and readers, here are a dozen quotes that help capture his fertile, febrile mind and his playfulness with words.[40]

1. A sure cure for seasickness is to sit under a tree.
2. How long was I in the army? Five foot eleven.
3. All I ask is the chance to prove that money can't make me happy.
4. At Victoria Station the RTO [Railway Transport Officer] gave me a travel warrant, a white feather and a picture of Hitler marked "This is your enemy." I searched every compartment but he wasn't on the train.—*Adolf Hitler—My Part in His Downfall.*
5. General: "Where are you from?" Milligan: "London." General: "Which part?" Milligan: "Well, all of me."
6. Any man can be 62, but it takes a bus to be 62A.
7. Education isn't everything; for a start it isn't an elephant.
8. A man loses his dog, so he puts an ad in the paper. And the ad says, "Here boy!"
9. Said Hamlet to Ophelia, "I'll draw a sketch of thee; what kind of pencil shall I use? 2B or not 2B?"
10. Chopsticks are one of the reasons the Chinese never invented custard.
11. Well, we can't stand around here doing nothing; people will think we're working.—*The Goon Show*
12. Announcer: Ten miles he swam—the last three were agony.
    Seagoon: They were over land. Finally I fell in a heap on the ground. I've no idea who left it there.—*The Goon Show*

---

[40] He once said, "I'm Irish. We think sideways."

Mixed Metaphors

Similar in some ways to **Malapropisms** and **Mondegreens**, these spoken or written aberrations betray often amusing results of muddled thought. They result from someone whose mind is grasping too quickly for creative images to anticipate what will happen when you string them together.

To whet our appetite, meet Boyle Roche (1736-1807), who offered this dazzling imagery in the Irish Parliament: "Mr. Speaker, I smell a rat. I see him floating in the air. But mark me, sir, I will nip him in the bud."

It's not without reason that someone described him as "the buffoon of the Conservative Party," a judgment supported by three more Boyle quotations:

- [...they] would cut us to mincemeat and throw our bleeding heads on that table to stare us in the face.
- All along the untrodden footpaths of the future, I can see the footprints of an unseen hand.
- The cup of Ireland's misery has been overflowing for centuries and is not yet half full.

***

For more contemporary examples an excellent resource is the thoughtco.com website,[41] from which we'll quietly purloin three concluding examples.

---

[41] https://www.thoughtco.com/what-are-mixed-metaphors-1691770.

- So now what we are dealing with is the rubber meeting the road, and instead of biting the bullet on these issues, we just want to punt.
- [T]he bill is mostly a stew of spending on existing programs, whatever their warts may be.
- The mayor has a heart as big as the Sahara for protecting "his" police officers, and that is commendable. Unfortunately, he also often strips his gears by failing to engage the clutch when shifting what emanates from his brain to his mouth. The bullets he fires too often land in his own feet.

Mnemonics

I first met Richard of York when I was in high school. It was clear from our first interaction that he was a typically eccentric Brit, as I suspect you'll agree. What I still remember half a century later is that *Richard of York Grew Bananas in Vienna*. To his credit, he helped me remember, for my science classes, the colors of the spectrum: Red-Orange-Yellow-Green-Blue-Indigo-Violet.

Mnemonics are memory devices, typically relying on a contrived sentence or sequence of letters to help someone recall a set of facts. Sometimes they're in the form of a rhyme or a song, as in this well-known example for remembering the days in the months:

Thirty days hath September, April, June, and November;
All the rest have thirty-one,
Save February, with twenty-eight days clear,
And twenty-nine each leap year.[42]

There's no limit to the areas where mnemonics can help us learn. You'll recognize this one from history:

In fourteen hundred ninety-two
Columbus sailed the ocean blue.

---

[42] I can't forego the opportunity to share the *Mad Magazine* parody, from 1952:
Thirty Days hath Septober,
April, June and no wonder.
All the rest have peanut butter except my grandmother.
She has a little red tricycle!

And from your English teacher, to steer you through some sticky spelling situations:

I before E except after C
Or when sounding like A
As in neighbor and weigh.

Then, moving on to arithmetic: If you're unsure of the order of operations, remember Aunt Sally. To get her help, *Please excuse my dear aunt Sally*, who will never let you forget this sequence:

- Parentheses
- Exponents
- Multiplication
- Division
- Addition
- Subtraction

***

The word mnemonic is derived from the Greek *mnemon* ("mindful"), which itself comes from the Greek word meaning "to remember." But there's an unanswered question about mnemonics and their usefulness. What if you can't remember if it's *Richard* of York? Is it Henry, George or Basil? What we need is another word that describes a memory trick for recalling a mnemonic.

(Still working on that; I'll get back to you.)

Moist

Many women will want to skip this entry, not because it contains material that will offend them, but because of the word itself. For reasons that aren't entirely clear, *moist* engenders in many women and teenage girls a sense of revulsion. Many of them apparently detest its connotations of bodily functions. This word regularly crops up as the one this group detests more than any other. The feelings about this word are so strong that I decided to use *moist* as the premise for my novel, *Never Say "Moist" at Wyndover College*, a satire about censorship on a college campus.

If you Google "What words do people dislike?" you'll find that *moist* has good company. Other words are *chunky, phlegm, secrete, squirt* and *tofu*.

Mondegreens

A Mondegreen results from mishearing something and interpreting it in a way that makes at least some sense to the hearer. Think of the little girl in church who heard the hymn lyrics, "Gladly the cross I'd bear" as "Gladly the cross-eyed bear."

Many come from mis-heard lyrics, as in the Creedence Clearwater Revival song, "Bad Moon on the Rise." The words "There's a bad moon on the rise" have been interpreted as "There's a bathroom on the right."

"Cry me a river" became "Crimean river" to at least one listener. The Beatles' song, "Lucy in the Sky with Diamonds" has this line: "The girl with kaleidoscope eyes." That got misperceived as "The girl with colitis goes by."

Unlike a malapropism, the use of a wrong but similar sounding word, a mondegreen is generated by the hearer of the word or phrase. It's a relatively new word, having been coined by author Sylvia Wright. When she was young she mis-heard the words of a Scottish ballad, "The Bonny Earl of Murray." The key verse for our purposes is:

Ye highlands and ye lowlands
Oh where hae you been?
Thou hae slay the Earl of Murray
And Lady Mondegreen.

At least, this is what she had heard. The actual wording of the last two lines was, "Thou hae slay the Earl of Murray and *laid him on the green.*" Wright coined the word to describe the misunderstood lyrics and mondegreen has since made its way into the language and now shows up in dictionaries too.

See also **Eggcorns**.

Mountweazel, Lillian Virginia (1942-1973)

Lillian Virginia Mountweazel and the word *esquivalience*, (meaning "the willful avoidance of one's official responsibilities") have the most unlikely of connections: Neither of them exists. At least, not outside their deliberate fabrication.

But first some background. Compilers of dictionaries and other reference works have a potential problem. One cannot copyright factual information, only the result of compiling it. For example, let's say I go to the trouble of compiling and publishing a list of all the election results (federal, state and local) in Alaska and Hawaii since they became US states. That's all factual information, available to anyone who's willing to track it down. But by itself this data cannot be copyrighted; what *can* is my compilation. However, if someone else wants to publish my work as his own, giving it a new title and changing the font and layout perhaps, and doing a different introduction, it's tough for me to prove my work was stolen. "Hey," this person says. "This is all factual information that's publicly accessible. I just gathered the same material you did."

And that's where Ms. Mountweazel and words like *esquivalience* come in. Publishers have long resorted to inserting fake information—such as the brief biography on the nonexistent Ms Mountweazel. She made her debut in the 1975 edition of the *New Columbia Encyclopedia*. The fictitious entry read:

> *Mountweazel, Lillian Virginia, 1942-1973, American photographer, b. Bangs, Ohio. Turning from fountain design to photography in 1963, Mountweazel produced her celebrated portraits of the South Sierra Miwok in 1964. She*

was awarded government grants to make a series of photo-essays of unusual subject matter, including New York City buses, the cemeteries of Paris and rural American mailboxes. The last group was exhibited extensively abroad and published as Flags Up! (1972) Mountweazel died at 31 in an explosion while on assignment for Combustibles magazine.

As far as is known, no one has brazenly copied that entry. But as one of the *Encyclopedia's* editors said, if anyone were to do so they would know. The same applied to the word *esquivalience*, which the compilers of the 2001 edition of the *New Oxford American Dictionary* set as a "copyright trap." Sure enough, it was picked up by Dictionary.com, which then dropped it when they realized the word's pedigree.

A similar result arose in another medium. British comedian and Monty Python star, John Cleese, mischievously inserted fabricated names of films into his *Who's Who* listing, such as *The Bonar Law Story*. He then took delight in seeing these cited in scholarly articles about him, including one in *The Encyclopedia of Television*.

Back to reality, where the esteemed Ms. Mountweazel has now earned her eponymous place in dictionaries as a legitimate word that, paradoxically, describes a bogus entry inserted specifically as a copyright trap.

If you'd like more examples of the phenomenon to which she has given her name, check out a 2012 article in *Mental Floss* titled "10 Hoax Definitions, Paper Towns, and Other Things That Don't Exist."[43]

---

[43] https://www.mentalfloss.com/article/30957/fun-copyright-traps-10-hoax-definitions-paper-towns-and-other-things-don%E2%80%99t-exist.

Mumpsimus—Shout It From The Rooftops

I don't remember how or precisely when I first encountered the word *mumpsimus*. But it was only a few years ago. Since then it has become one of my favorites, joining the ranks of *acnestis*, *defenestration*, *steatopygous* and *ucalegon*.[44] No, it's not because they're long and fancy sounding words. Rather, *mumpsimus* appeals for six reasons.

1. It's a sharply focused word. It means "someone who clings to an error despite all the evidence that the person is wrong." Unlike the word *set*, which is the English word with most meanings,[45] both as a noun and a verb, *mumpsimus* zeroes in on a particular situation with sharp, clear definition. The word is like a Navy SEAL attack on an enemy target, with a laser focus in its meaning.

2. *Mumpsimus* has a fascinating origin. Unlike many words whose origin is obscure or unknown, *mumpsimus'* genesis is well established. The word comes from a Catholic priest who mangled the Latin wording in saying the Mass. When he should have said "sumpsimus," meaning "we have received," after the Eucharist, he said *mumpsimus* (which is meaningless) instead. Even though the error was

---

[44] *Acnestis*—Itching on a part of the body where one cannot scratch, usually between the shoulder blades.
Defenestration—The act of throwing someone out a window.
Steatopygous—Having fat buttocks.
Ucalegon—A neighbor whose house is on fire or has burned down.
[45] See **Oddities**.

repeatedly pointed out to him, he refused to correct his wording.

3. When I first encountered *mumpsimus* I read a story that illustrated its meaning. A mental patient insists that he is dead. His psychiatrist asks him, "Do dead men bleed?" The patient says, "No." So the doctor takes a needle and pricks the patient's finger and a drop of blood oozes out. The patient looks at his finger in wonderment and says, "Wow, so dead men *do* bleed."

4. I love the sound of it. No, it's not an onomatopoeic word, like *buzz* or *plop* or *borborygmous* (meaning tummy rumbles). But just saying it aloud, with an emphasis on the first syllable, *mump*-simus, is for reasons I cannot explain immensely gratifying.

5. The unusualness of the word leads me, at least for a moment, to reflect in wonder once again at the richness of the English language and its unending capacity to delight me with one surprise after another. Now and again we meet a new word, which we realize is a perfect fit for a particular need. And we are tempted to say, "Thank you, English, for giving this to me."

6. Finally, there's the word's utility. Perhaps that's the most important point of all. Mark Twain said, "The difference between the almost right word and the right word is really a large matter. It's the difference between the lightning bug and the lightning." *Mumpsimus* is the perfect word to describe certain people who, for whatever motives, refuse to accept the facts. They may do so out of habit, like the priest getting the wording wrong. That was his way of doing things and by golly he wasn't going to change. Or it may be that the prospect of needing to change is so threatening that one clings to an incorrect view of reality instead. Think of climate-change deniers, for example.

Mumpsimus, I contend, is a word for our times. It's time to push it to the front in our conversations and public discourse. Put it in headlines, write it into contracts, shout it from the rooftops.

Names

No words have more immediate importance to us than our names. They are intensely personal. We could explore here numerous aspects about our names:

- How people select names for their children.
- The meaning of names.
- Which names are currently most popular with parents. Babynames.com lists Oliver, Liam and Ethan as the most favored boys' names at the beginning of 2020. Topping the girls' list are Charlotte, Ava and Amelia/Emilia.
- Why people change their names, including the names that now-famous celebrities selected to make them more marketable. Think of Bob Dylan (Robert Alan Zimmerman); John Denver (Henry John Deutschendorf Jr.); Cary Grant (Archibald Leach); Elton John (Reginald Kenneth Dwight); and Marilyn Monroe (Norma Jeane Mortenson).
- The legal basis on which children can change embarrassing names, or the power of governments to forbid certain names. In New Zealand, for example, you would not be allowed to name your child "Lucifer." In Sweden, "Ikea" is out as your baby's name.

***

Instead of beginning a doctoral-dissertation length study of these and other aspects of names, we'll focus only on this final topic: embarrassing names. The New Zealand authorities, in addition to banning Lucifer in 2008, needed to consider the case of a nine-year-old girl. According to a BBC report, she was made a ward of the court so that she could legally change her given name: Talula Does The Hula From Hawaii.[46] The judge in the case said, "The court is profoundly concerned about the very poor judgment which this child's parents have shown in choosing this name." He added, "It makes a fool of the child and sets her up with a social disability and handicap, unnecessarily." The girl's new name was not made known.

New Zealand officials blocked other names given by creative (or possibly demented) parents: Sex Fruit, Fat Boy, Cinderella Beauty Blossom and, for twins, Fish and Chips. Oddly though, the names Violence and Number 16 Bus Shelter were permitted.

The BBC invited responses to its article, one of which came from Ftango Molasses, from London. She[47] said, "I hated my parents for what they named me up until I was a teenager, but then I just became comfortable with it. I suppose it was just bad for me as my sister was called Judy."

My favorite response in the article came from someone who wrote, "No-one ever considered that the child might like the quirkiness of their name. Nothing has ever held back my development or progress in the world. I'm now working in the catering trade and everyone calls me Eggy. I don't see the problem." His name? Egnorwiddle Waldstrom.

But even Eggy pales when placed next to some of those listed by Bill Bryson in *The Mother Tongue*, in the chapter on names.[48]

---

[46] The names in this entry are all taken from the BBC report titled "NZ judge orders 'odd' name change." Google that title if you're skeptical. Or Google it for some more encounters with parents of very small brain.

[47] I am assuming Ftango is a "she" but as this is a far from common name it's hard to be sure.

[48] Bryson also notes that "[T]he British pronounce their names in ways that bear almost no resemblance to their spelling. Levenson-Gower is 'looson gore,' Majoribanks is 'marchbanks,' Hiscox is

Among several examples he cites, he mentions "the truly unbeatable Leone Sextus Denys Oswolf Fraduati Tollemache-Tollemache-de-Orellana-Plantagenet-Tollemache-Tollemache, a British army major who died in World War I."

Unbeatable, indeed—in real life, that is. We should, however, pay homage to the Monty Python crew for their invented name of that great musical composer,

Johann Gambolputty de von Ausfern-schplenden-schlitter-crasscrenbon-fried-digger-dingle-dangle-dongle-dungle-burstein-von-knacker-thrasher-apple-banger-horowitz-ticolensic-grander-knotty-spelltinkle-grandlich-grumblemeyer-spelterwasser-kurstlich-himbleeisen-bahnwagen-gutenabend-bitte-ein-nürnburger-bratwustle-gerspurten-mitzweimache-luber-hundsfut-gumberaber-shönendanker-kalbsfleisch-mittler-aucher von Hautkopft of Ulm.

***

Hmmm.... I think if I had to choose a favorite, I'd still go with Egnorwiddle.

'hizzko,' Howick is 'hoyk,' Ruthven is 'rivven,' Zuill is 'yull,' Menzies is 'mingiss.'"

Non-Sequiturs

I may be slow but I like non-sequiturs.
   —Unknown

A non-sequitur is a thing of nonsense, and potentially a source of much amusement. We're talking about two or more sets of words connected to each other in a way that doesn't follow. That's what the Latin means: "It does not follow." For example, "Born in Alabama, he was the first in his family to graduate from college." How do these two parts connect, you ask? They don't.

Theodore Bernstein, author of *The Careful Writer*, says if pieces of information are placed close together, they should also be close in meaning. He gives as an example: "Born in Glasgow, he loved his mother." The sentence suggests that it was because he was born in that city that he loved Mom—and perhaps *only* because he was born there. (What if he'd been born Aberdeen or Edinburgh? Would he still have loved her?) By contrast, Bernstein says this sentence would make sense: "Born in Glasgow, he had no trouble learning to play the bagpipes." Here we have two pieces of information that might well be related, Glasgow being a better place than most to learn this instrument.[49]

Non sequiturs are often used as a device in comedy or theatre of the absurd. In a comedic moment in *Hamlet*, for example, Shakespeare has this exchange:

---

[49] Question: Why do you usually see bagpipers marching while playing?
Answer: It's harder to hit a moving target.

Polonius: If you call me Jephthah, my lord, I have a daughter that I love passing well.
Hamlet: Nay, that follows not.

Here Hamlet calls Polonius on an obvious non sequitur. Watch for them; they proliferate especially in the election season when politicians forsake logic even more readily than usual.

Oddities

The letter A—If you start spelling out numbers (1, 2, 3...), you wouldn't use the letter A until you reach a *thousand*.

***

AEIOU words—English has a handful for words with each vowel, in order, once only. Here, with brief definitions, are six of them.

- *Abstemious*— Eating and drinking in moderation.
- *Annelidous*— Of the nature of an annelid or worm.
- *Arsenious*—Related to arsenic.
- *Arterious*—Related to arteries.
- *Caesious*—Bluish or grayish green.
- *Facetious*— Playfully jocular; humorous.

Or how about backwards? Yes, we can do that too:

- *Duoliteral*— Consisting of two letters only.
- *Subcontinental*—Pertaining to a large land mass, that is separate to some degree but still part of a continent.
- *Uncomplimentary*—Just what it sounds like.

***

Almost—The longest commonly used word in the English language with all the letters in alphabetical order.

***

Angry and *hungry*—The only common words in English that end in -gry.

***

Asthma and *isthmi* (the plural of *isthmus*)—The only six-letter words that begin and end with a vowel and have no other vowels in between.

***

Bookkeeping—Can you find any other words with three double letters in a row?

***

Cushion and *fashion*—The only English words that end in -shion. Others have the same sound, like *tension*. But that's not the same....

***

Dermatoglyphics, meaning "the study of skin markings." One of the few fifteen-letter words that has no letter repeated. See also *Uncopyrightable*.

***

Dreamt—The only English word that ends in the letters MT.

***

Flammable and *Inflammable*. A rare word pair of identical synonyms. There may be subtle nuances in how we use them differently but on the face of it one of these words should have driven the other out of existence. Hasn't happened. Same with *habitable* and *inhabitable*.

***

Forty—The only number which has its letters in alphabetical order.

***

Monosyllabic—As the saying goes, "Monosyllabic isn't."

***

Nice would be a strong contender in the English Language Flexible Meaning competition, if there were such a thing. Merriam-Webster notes that it "has had an astonishing range of meanings over the years, including *coy, wanton, neat* and *trivial.*"

***

Queueing—The only word with five consecutive vowels.

***

Rhythms—One of the longest words with no regular vowels.

***

Set—This word is credited by *The Guinness Book of Records* with having the most meanings, fifty-eight as a noun, 126 as a verb, and ten as a participial adjective.[50]

***

---

[50] As noted by Paul Dickson in *Dickson's Word Treasury.*

Stewardesses—The longest word that can be typed with only the left hand.

***

Therein—A seven-letter word that contains thirteen words spelled using consecutive letters: the, he, her, er, here, I, there, ere, rein, re, in, therein, and herein. (If you're suspicious about the status of *er*, it's OK. Merriam-Webster accepts it as an interjection, usually indicating hesitation.)

***

Uncopyrightable—See *Dermatoglyphics*.

***

Underground—One of only two words beginning and ending in -*und*. The other is *underfund*.

Only: An Exercise

Where you place a word in a sentence can dramatically change the meaning. Here's an example: "I hit him in the eye yesterday." Now let's insert the word only, in different places, and see what happens:

- *Only* I hit him in the eye yesterday. *I alone got to clobber the guy.*
- I *only* hit him in the eye yesterday. *I was tempted to poke him with a bamboo stick but settled for only hitting him.*
- I hit *only* him in the eye yesterday. *Tempted though I was to hit his grandmother as well, I hit only him.*
- I hit him *only* in the eye yesterday. *His entire body was available but I went only for his eye.*
- I hit him in the *only* eye yesterday. *Poor fellow; he has only one eye and now its swollen shut.*
- I hit him in the eye *only* yesterday. *Ah, I remember it fondly.*
- I hit him in the eye yesterday *only*. *No, your honor, the allegation that I hit him each day last week is untrue; it was just that one day.*

Onomatopoeia

These are words that sound like their meanings. Here are some familiar ones:

- *Babble*
- *Bam*
- *Gurgle*
- *Mumble*
- *Slam*
- *Splash*
- *Warble*
- *Zap*

You can add to these a virtually endless list of animal noises: *oink, quack, woof.* But my list wouldn't be complete without *borborygmous*, meaning tummy rumbles. (This one got a mention in **Mumpsimus** but I see no harm repeating it here.)

***

Of course, English has no monopoly on onomatopoeic words. *The Meaning of Tingo,* by Adam Jacot de Boinod (see **The Desert Island Bookshelf**), offers several examples from his scouring of dozens of dictionaries of other languages. Herewith three examples:

- Phut (Vietnamese): the noise of string or rope that snaps
- Vuhubya-hubya (from Tsonga, in South Africa): the flapping of pendulous breasts of a woman hurrying

- Zhaghzhagh (Persian): the noise made by almonds or by other nuts shaken together in a bag

***

And to conclude, a joke: A man goes to the doctor who examines him and says, "Well, you've got high blood pressure, indigestion and onomatopoeia."

And the man says, "Well, I understand high blood pressure and indigestion. But what's onomatopoeia?"

And the doctor says, "Just what it sounds like."

George Orwell

George Orwell, best known for his novels *1984* and *Animal Farm*, was a meticulous writer, who fortunately also left us with enduring advice on using words well. In an essay titled "Politics and the English Language," he decried the mushy, fuzzy and dishonest language that he said had crept into political discourse. This 1946 commentary and set of suggestions remains as valuable more than seventy years later as it was then, which is why writing teachers continue to steer their students toward it.

If one reads nothing else, Orwell's six rules with which he concludes his advice are invaluable. Here they are:

1. Never use a metaphor, simile or other figure of speech which you are used to seeing in print.
2. Never use a long word where a short one will do.
3. If it is possible to cut a word out, always cut it out.
4. Never use the passive where you can use the active.
5. Never use a foreign phrase, a scientific word or a jargon word if you can think of an everyday English equivalent.
6. Break any of these rules sooner than say anything outright barbarous.

Elsewhere in the essay Orwell cites a passage from the book of Ecclesiastes, in the Old Testament: "I returned and saw under the sun, that the race is not to the swift, nor the battle to the strong, neither yet bread to the wise, nor yet riches to men of understanding, nor yet favor to men of skill, but time and chance happeneth to them all."

Then he rewrites this in what he describes as "modern English of the worst sort":

"Objective considerations of contemporary phenomena compel the conclusion that success or failure in competitive activities exhibits no tendency to be commensurate with innate capacity, but that a considerable element of the unpredictable must invariably be taken into account."

Ough Words

If you're a native English speaker be grateful you don't have to learn from scratch our language's often bizarre irregularities and inconsistencies. Bill Bryson notes in *The Mother Tongue* that "No other language in the world has more words spelled the same way and yet pronounced differently."

Let's look at the issue of pronunciation of the letters "ough." What possible explanation can you give to an English-language learner for saying....

- *Cough* as "coff"
- *Dough* as "doe"
- *Drought* as "drout"
- *Hiccough* as "hikkup"
- *Hough* as "hock" (*Hough* as a noun is admittedly obscure and unlikely ever to be encountered by your ESL student; it's the Scottish word for what the English call the "hock," the joint in the hind leg of an animal like a cow or horse—corresponding to an ankle on a person. It also means hamstringing an animal. If your student reads the Authorized, or King James, version of the Bible, however, he or she will find it used four times as a verb in the Old Testament, twice in Joshua chapter 11.)
- *Plough* as "plow"
- *Rough* as "ruff"
- *Thoroughfare* as "thur-eh-fare"
- *Through* as "throo"
- *Thought* as "thawt"

There are a few more, if you really want to punish yourself (or your student), although these are typically place names.

Oxymorons

Oxymorons, statements that are self-contradictory, fall into two categories. The first is the pure oxymoron, perhaps an unintentional statement that literally contradicts itself. For example, to say something is *pretty ugly* or a *little big* makes no sense. Others are:

- *Friendly fire*
- *Only choice*
- *A silent scream*
- *Terribly good*
- *Peacekeeping force*
- *Virtual reality*

One of my favorites is *The voices of the voiceless*. We are so used to hearing some of these expressions that we no longer recognize them as the oxymorons they are.

The second type are those contrived to poke fun at or deliberately insult a group of people or a concept. Examples here include the well-known *ethical lawyers* and *military intelligence*. How valid these are is a matter of opinion; all the lawyers I have met over the years have been decent and ethical people (as far as I could tell). But this second category provides boundless opportunities for taking a dig at unpopular groups. Here are a few that are intentionally barbed:

- *American culture*
- *Caring Republican*
- *Frugal Democrat*
- *Government worker*
- *Marital bliss*

For a definitive, and always growing, list of oxymorons, take a look at this website: www.oxymoronlist.com and load up on insults for your next friendly fight. (While you're at it, take a look at **Harsh Words** if you haven't already.)

Palindromes

I first recall encountering a palindrome in a history class in school, where Lord Glenelg (1778-1866) surfaced. The teacher pointed out the name Glenelg is spelled the same forward and backward. He was a Scottish politician and colonial administrator but I didn't remember that bit (I had to look it up). All I recall was the marvel of having a name that could be read either way.

Palindromes are one of those word categories that are fun to play with but have no other inherent value. There are lots of them in English. It's said that the first palindrome was uttered in the Garden of Eden, when Adam first met Eve: "Madam, I'm Adam."

The shortest palindromes are of course only three letters; you can't have a two-word palindrome unless you count a double letter word like *aa*, which Wiktionary defines as "A form of lava flow associated with Hawaiian-type volcanoes." But that feels like cheating, so we move on to three-letter words such as *pap*, *pep*, *pip*, *pop*, *pup*—and that's working with just the letter P.

We work our way up to four letters: *peep* (sticking with P....). But the longest English palindrome begins with (and ends with, of course), the letter R: *redivider*. Not exactly an everyday word, but it qualifies for the gold medal.

Other impressive single-word palindromes are *deified*, *racecar*, *repaper*, *reviver* and *rotator*.

There are palindromic sentences too. Many examples visibly strain to follow the rules, such as *Sums are not set as a test on Erasmus*. Hard to imagine anyone saying this in conversation. Still, it follows the rule. So does the one imagining what

Napoleon would have said before his exile to Elba: *Able was I ere I saw Elba.* It takes quite the imagination to think of this deposed French-speaking leader coming up with English palindromic sentences. But we'll leave it at that. (Although, let's switch for a moment to another European language, German, with its delightfully palindromic word *eibohphobie*—which means a fear of palindromes.)

Let's give the last word to a palindrome that makes sense and tells a story: *A man, a plan, a canal—Panama!* Clever.

To be honest, though, I prefer the parody: *A man, a plan, a canal—Suez!*

Pangrams

A pangram is a sentence or passage that contains all the letters of the alphabet. The shorter the pangram, the more impressive it is. Coming in at 33 letters, the best known is *The quick brown fox jumps over a lazy dog.*

Can we do any better? Yes: *Pack my box with five dozen liquor jugs.* (32 letters)

Both these pangrams make sense. To do even better you need to start verging on more fanciful constructions or introducing proper names, as in these examples:

The five boxing wizards jump quickly. (31 letters)

Waltz, nymph, for quick jigs vex Bud. (28 letters)

We are approaching the "Perfect Pangram" of just 26 letters, each letter of the alphabet, and no more. Can we get there?

These examples are taken from Gyles Brandreth's book, *The Joy of Lex*, which includes this Perfect Pangram—although admittedly contrived to the point of blatantly self-serving artificiality:

J. Q. Schwartz flung D. V. Pike my box. (26 letters; drum roll please, with a trumpet or two as well).

***

Pangrams also appear, unintentionally, in writing. Here's the shortest one from the Harry Potter series. It appears in J. K. Rowling's *Harry Potter and the Deathly Hallows*. Dumbledore says: *"Nice job, I hope? Pleasant? Easy? Sort of thing you'd expect an unqualified wizard kid to be able to do without overstretching themselves?"* (110 letters)

Rowling was far more economical than Shakespeare, whose shortest pangram, from *The Merchant of Venice*, has 157 letters.

> *Lorenzo: Hold here, take this: tell gentle Jessica*
> *I will not fail her; speak it privately.*
> *Go, gentlemen.*
> Exit Launcelot
> *Will you prepare you for this masque tonight?*
> *I am provided of a torchbearer.*

For more fun with pangrams, go to wordsmith.org/pangram.

Personal Word Blunders

I remember the moment clearly: I was in the graduate school lounge at Wheaton College, a leading Christian institution, in fall 1974, working on a project. Across the table from me was Arlene, another student whom I'd got to know in my first few months on campus. We were on friendly terms.

Then came the question, which forever changed my assumptions about American English, and no doubt her assumptions about me. I asked her, "Arlene, do you have a rubber?"

She was astonished. Instantly, I knew why. All good South African boys who went to the United States, and especially to Wheaton, were made aware of the difference between *rubber* and *eraser*. And presumably all bad boys were even more familiar with that distinction. Nothing had prepared me for a moment of such awkwardness. All I could mutter as a follow-up to her stunned silence was something like, "Don't worry, I'll find one somewhere else." Then, as I recall, I left the room. (What followed isn't quite as clear; I think my memory was at that point functioning in modest PTSD-mode.)

It was a wake-up call. Until then, I had fitted in just fine—or thought I had. I expected the Americans with whom I was surrounded to have accents, as they kept saying I did. I was prepared by movies for the fact that Americans drive on the wrong side of the road. And I knew of the vocabulary differences. (See **British vs American English**.) But my own culture and vocabulary were so imbedded that it was just a matter of time before an Arlene moment would arrive. My *rubber/eraser* episode showed me I needed to be far more alert in my new linguistic milieu than I realized.

Arlene, if you're out there, and by any chance reading this…
I am sorry.

***

Another cultural gap emerged when a friend and I were MC-ing a variety concert at the university where I taught. Somehow in the banter in front of the curtain I found myself needing to say an unfamiliar word, at least with respect to its pronunciation: *calliope*. I'd seen it in print but couldn't recall hearing it. So my best shot was referring to a kalli-OPE, to the puzzlement of my fellow-MC and no doubt the audience as well. Behind the curtains during the next sketch he set me straight: it's pronounced ke-LIE-o-pee. We needed to cover for my ignorance so the next time we emerged for our continuity announcements and introductions, he asked me why I'd said the word that way. So I told the story about President Kennedy, who was once asked why some Americans pronounced *schedule* as shed-ule and others said sked-ule. He answered[51] that "It all depends which shool you went to."

---

[51] Supposedly. I have not been able to confirm this story.

Pet Peeves

The entries below supplement those in the **Errors List** and **The Right Word**. The difference is that the words or usage issues highlighted here for some reason trigger in me a tangible level of annoyance or irritation. Every time I encounter one of these items my irritation is reinforced. These pet peeves, then, unlike other pets, should be shunned, not nurtured, and starved to death, not fed.

***

Cliché—When used as an adjective, as in "His thinking is so cliché." Cliché, my friends, is a *noun*. You wouldn't write "Her performance was dull and wood." You'd say "wooden." So you would need "His thinking is so clichéd."

***

Could care less—What people intend to say is "I couldn't care less," meaning "I already care so little about this issue that it's not possible for me to care any less." To say that "I could care less" indicates you haven't yet reached bottom. Avoid this illogical expression.

***

Criterion/Criteria—The first is singular, the second is plural. "The only criterion he used in voting for president was the color of the candidate's hair" vs "My top two criteria in hiring an au pair are the lack of a criminal background and an ability to teach my four-year-old Latin."

***

Different—As in "Last summer we visited five different countries in Europe." I am glad you made clear they were different. On our trip we visit only three different ones but another four that were all exactly the same. Can you believe it? Four identical countries....

***

Double check—A fantasy....

"Good morning; I want to confirm that my information is current."

"Sure, I'll be glad to help. Let me double-check that for you."

"You mean *check*. You haven't checked yet so how could you *double*-check? You can *double*-check only after you've checked once already. *Double* in this context means check twice, doesn't it?"

"Oh."

***

Eat healthy—This grating expression is increasingly accepted as normal, especially among certain good-food zealots. But it's still wrong. *Healthy* is an adjective. "She is a healthy child" or "We eat healthy food." We need an adverb to elaborate on our way of eating: "Eat healthily." We wouldn't say "We ate our wheat germ and granola *quick*." No, it would be *quickly*. Grumble grumble.

***

Feel—I know I am not alone in objecting to sentences like "I feel that Shakespeare is overrated as a playwright." Two problems. The first is that I am not *feeling* that. I may *think* that or *believe* that. So the first problem is that there's a sloppiness of word choice, common though this usage may be.

The second problem is more subtle. Whether I intend to or not, I am shielding myself from any possible disagreement or even discussion. If I say, "I feel tired/angry/melancholy," you can't dispute that. Maybe I don't seem that way to you. But how can you contradict what I say I am feeling? My feelings are what they are. However, if I extend this subjectivity to something that could be discussed objectively (like the merits of Shakespeare's plays), you can make excellent arguments about Shakespeare's merits—and I have the ultimate comeback. "Well, I just feel they're not that good." I am using a preemptive defense mechanism against any argument you may raise. How can you dispute my feelings? My students didn't easily grasp the implications of misusing *feel* and the importance of making their thinking available to testing.

***

Final Descent—You know the routine. As our flight approaches its end, our cheery flight attendant tells us to be sure our seats are in the upright position, our seat belts are fastened, and so on. But these instructions are often coupled with the news that we will soon begin our "final descent." Now we're puzzled: How many other descents have we had so far? Just one? Or perhaps two or three? And why weren't we told about those?

Why not just say "descent"? Grumble grumble.

***

Necessarily—When it's missing, as in those earnest warnings at the beginning of movies that say "the views expressed here do not represent those of MegaTransGlobalCorp Inc and its affiliates." So, if the views expressed champion motherhood, apple pie and teddy bears, the disclaimer is saying that MegaTransGlobalCorp (and its affiliates) opposes these cherished concepts. No matter the views expressed, the company does not embrace them. No, no, no: what they want is "do not *necessarily* represent..." That's the weasel language they need to ward off any complaint about the movie's portrayal of motherhood, apple pie and teddy bears. With "not necessarily," MegaTransGlobalCorp can say, "Maybe we're for them, maybe we're not." Which is what they meant to say in the beginning.

***

Predominantly/Predominately—As in "The audience were *predominately* children." The problem here is that the writer wants *predominantly*, an adjective, like the root word, *dominant*. *Predominate* is a verb, like *dominate. The Chicago Manual of Style* says, "Using *predominate* as an adjective is common but loose usage—and the adverb *predominately* (for the correct *predominantly*) is likely to make the literary person's teeth hurt." Yet one sees this error often, most recently on the website of a publisher whom I was considering approaching to publish this book. No longer.

***

Thanks to—As in "Thanks to a bout of food poisoning he missed the Rolling Stones concert." Oh, thank you, thank you, great god of food poisoning, for inflicting these days of misery on me, and making me miss The Stones....

I admit I am on weak ground here. Some dictionaries are clear that *thank* conveys both the sense of gratitude and causality or responsibility. Wiktionary says *thanks to* can mean: "*Because of*, normally used with a positive connotation, though it can be used sarcastically." And *The Chambers Dictionary* notes the meaning, "To hold responsible for something." The example it gives is "He has only himself to thank for this mess." But it's the negative association in examples like the food poisoning sentence that continue to jar. Am I alone in feeling this way? Any hope of a support group here?

***

Too—Two problems here. The first arises in uses like *too much, too hot, too late*. These usages are tautologies, verbal statements in the form "X equals X." A sentence like "Don't eat too much" is offering meaningless advice. By definition, *too much* in this setting means "a quantity so great that it is a bad thing." In ordinary conversation, this can be innocent enough. But as author Robert Thouless points out[52] a tautology can be a trap in the language of argument. An example he gives is someone saying, "You will admit that too much freedom in schools is a bad thing." He points out that this tautology is not a factual statement; it is saying "a bad thing is a bad thing." Yet someone asked to respond to the statement about "too much freedom in schools" nevertheless feels compelled to agree. After all, *too much* of anything is bad, right? This problem with *too* is similar to the profound advice we get on some food packaging, especially for frozen items: "Do not overheat." Well *duh*.... Of *course* you shouldn't heat it more than you should heat it.

Problem no. 2: Take for example the wording, "Too many people are dying in road accidents." This implies that there's a lower number of deaths that would be just fine. Maybe a charitable interpretation of this usage is that it is inevitable we will have some deaths on the roads. And although we can't define that number, all the deaths above that number make for "too many." Maybe. Still, it doesn't sit right to read that "too many children died of malnutrition last year." I can't escape the barbaric conclusion that there was somehow an acceptable or tolerable number.

---

[52] In a book on logic and arguments, *Straight and Crooked Thinking*.

***

Unnamed—As in, "Police arrested an unnamed 47-year-old man for burglary." The man is 47 years old and still doesn't have a name? Poor fellow. The word should be *unidentified*. Or reword it to say the police did not release the man's name.

Political Correctness

If you give me six lines written by the hand of the most honest of men, I will find something in them which will hang him.
   —Cardinal Richelieu

It wouldn't take six lines in this entry before something arises that someone will demand needs correction, rejection or possibly even hanging. Some readers will view this section as too soft on what they see as the excesses of PC; others may well see my criticisms as betraying my own bigotry and ignorance of deep issues that I just gloss over or treat too glibly.

[We've made it to about line six; any calls for a Richelieu-style hanging yet? No? Then let's move on.]

Henry Beard and Christopher Cerf, who compiled *The Official Politically Correct Dictionary and Handbook*, offer this definition of "politically correct": "Culturally sensitive; multiculturally unexceptionable; appropriately inclusive. The term 'politically correct,' co-opted by the white power elite as a tool for attacking multiculturalism, is no longer 'politically correct.'" As you might expect, this poses a paradox: how are we to talk about a term that, according to Beard and Cerf, it would be inappropriate to talk about? Still, we'll give it a shot.

Let's begin with an important aside. I normally think of "PC" as a progressive/liberal/political left phenomenon. I suspect most people apply the PC label that way. But there's a similar but opposing mindset, complete with vocabulary and expectations, on the political right.

The political right's approach to political correctness is equally ideological and self-assured of its cause. Writer Alex Nowrasteh wrote in *The Washington Post* that

[C]onservatives have their own, nationalist version of PC, their own set of rules regulating speech, behavior and acceptable opinions. I call it 'patriotic correctness.' It's a full-throated, un-nuanced, uncompromising defense of American nationalism, history and cherry-picked ideals. Central to its thesis is the belief that nothing in America can't be fixed by more patriotism enforced by public shaming, boycotts and policies to cut out foreign and non-American influences.

As part of a "patriotically correct" vocabulary, he said, one must for example refer to "illegals," illegal immigrant" or "illegal alien" to describe individuals who have broken immigration laws.

Then, in a different arena, if you were active in a fundamentalist church or attending a conservative Christian college, you would be expected to speak in terms of *pro-life* rather than *pro-choice*—and no doubt corrected if you didn't. And you would counter *reducing fossil fuel dependence*, a progressive rallying cry, with the *war on coal*. Vocabulary, in right wing circles, is no less important than among those in the progressive camp.

The reality, though, is that we typically don't refer to these views as constituting political correctness. So the comments that follow will focus on those wording issues associated with the progressive or politically left segments of Western society. From here on, then, PC will refer only to that side of the spectrum.

***

The most positive justification I've heard for PC is this: It's a matter of good manners. If I'm chatting with you I should not knowingly use words that will needlessly offend you. Politeness requires I be sensitive to your sensibilities. Moreover, in humility I need to recognize that I do not necessarily know what your sensibilities are and that I might inadvertently offend you in some way.[53]

The most positive contribution of PC proponents on the left has been to alert English speakers of some of the inherent biases in our language, for example, against women, minority groups, or developing nations. In so doing, feminism and other movements have identified language issues many of us previously ignored but about which we are now more sensitive. And we are better off because of it.

Especially when interacting with someone of a different cultural background, I need to be particularly attentive to my "word manners." But even as I try to mind my manners, PC language raises concerns. I'll identify four that trouble me.

***

The first is the easiest target and one that threatens whatever good is accomplished by champions of PC: the sheer silliness of people who want to change our vocabularies, coupled with the ostracism and condemnation that follow if you don't go along with the prescribed underlying ideology. I'm fine with inclusive language that favors *mail carrier* rather than *mailman* or *firefighter* rather than *fireman*. But then we've been offered as an alternative to *woman* such constructions as *wofem* or *wimyn*, or *overimony* instead of *testimony* (based on *ovary* rather than *testicle*).[54] Or instead of *dead* we have *terminally inconvenienced*. The fact that these proposed improvements or corrections haven't caught on doesn't detract from their silliness. No matter the good intentions of those seeking to formulate these words and phrases, and no matter how

---

[53] This is a good place to mention the concept of a *micro-aggression*, which Merriam-Webster defines as "a comment or action that subtly and often unconsciously or unintentionally expresses a prejudiced attitude toward a member of a marginalized group (such as a racial minority)."

[54] Several of these examples are taken from the now somewhat dated Beard and Cerf book.

appealing they are to those people who agree with them, the rest of us just find them ridiculous.

Likewise with more recent examples, such as the Seattle school referring to Easter eggs as "spring spheres" to avoid offending children who don't celebrate Easter. Or how about the San Francisco Board of Supervisors, which in 2019 issued a statement calling for felons who had completed their prison terms to be "rebranded," either as "returning residents" or "former justice-involved persons." Two final examples, from Britain. The Tunbridge Wells Borough Council in Kent banned the term "brainstorming" and replaced it with "thought showers" to avoid possible offense to epileptics.[55] Finally, an English job center rejected a recruiter's ad seeking "reliable" and "hard-working" applicants because it could be offensive to unreliable and lazy people.

***

A second and more substantive concern is the arrogance and self-righteousness that accompanies much of what I've seen in PC-land. We're talking about an attitude that flows from what essayist and literature professor Joseph Epstein condemned as the "virtucrat" mentality. He invented the term and first used it in an article for *The New York Times Magazine*. He defined a virtucrat as "any man or woman who is certain that his or her political views are not merely correct but deeply, morally righteous in the bargain."

The result is a "take-no-prisoners" approach to all aspects of life that are deemed to be politically charged—even though many of us may fail to see any problem with Easter eggs or "brainstorming." At their worst, PC proponents brook no dissent—thus leading George Carlin, the comedian cited several

---

[55] Of course, one wonders if the word "epileptics" doesn't carry an unwarranted stigma and whether that too should be euphemized. Maybe at a future council meeting.

other times in this book, to say that "Political Correctness is fascism pretending to be manners."

***

A third, and similar problem I see as clearly linked to a PC mindset is the bullying and stifling of unwelcome expression that now characterizes what's become known as the "cancel culture." Far from upholding another person's right to free expression, many students on college campuses now believe passionately that they have a lock on truth and are thus qualified to ban from speaking anyone whose views don't fit the prevailing ideology. That is why comedians like Jerry Seinfeld and Chris Rock now refuse to perform on college campuses. An article in *The Atlantic* in 2015 reported on the annual convention where comedians and other performers auditioned for students from hundreds of colleges and universities seeking to book entertainers. The writer said of these students that:

> *[A]lmost all of them have internalized the code that you don't laugh at politically incorrect statements; you complain about them. In part, this is because they are the inheritors of three decades of identity politics, which have come to be a central driver of attitudes on college campuses. But there's more to it than that. These kids aren't dummies; they look around their colleges and see that there are huge incentives to join the ideological bandwagon and harsh penalties for questioning the platform's core ideas.*

PC, in its most aggressive forms, asserts a particular ideological stance, one promoted so fervently that anyone countering it—or merely calling for other voices to be given a hearing—is deemed the enemy.

***

My fourth concern troubles me most. It is what I'd call a gutless reluctance to offend even those most deserving condemnation. Hence the notion of calling a bank robber *ethically disoriented* or *morally different.* "I'm not saying his action was right or wrong; after all, who am I to judge his value system? It's merely different from mine." This reluctance to offend takes the good contributions of **Euphemisms** to absurd levels, like describing as *differently abled* someone who is plain incompetent. Rather than seeking speech marked by kindness or inclusivity, PC thinking can lead to a self-deluding denial of truth and reality.

***

Much more that could be said but I'm already way past the number of lines Richelieu said he needed to find a reason to hang someone. Anyway, I need to go; I see there's a line of people forming at my front door. Wonder what they could want?

POSH—An Awakening

When I first heard the origin of the word *posh* (maybe in my teens or twenties), my world felt just a bit more orderly. One more unknown was now explained.... And it was a good story too: How more affluent people sailing from England to India would insist on a cabin on the port side of the ship on the outward journey, to protect them from the heat. Then, on the return journey, they would want the opposite: starboard on the way home. In other words, Port Out, Starboard Home, or POSH. It's a great word for describing, with a hint of distaste for, or resentment at, affluence and snobbery, the behavior of the upper classes who have money to burn.

But then the doubts began to creep in. I read here and there that there was no evidence to support this supposed etymology. Surely not: This was a story I *wanted* to believe. How could it not be true? Finally, I encountered the strongest argument against it yet, in a book by one of my favorite word people, Michael Quinion.[56]

According to this supposed scenario, the Peninsular and Oriental Steamship Company, or P&O, stamped wealthy passengers' tickets with POSH to show their status. "The trouble is," Quinion writes, "there is absolutely no evidence for it and P&O flatly denies any such term existed. It's just a legend, though a very persistent one." Nobody has even produced a ticket with such a stamp, or any other evidence to support this story.

---

[56] For the record, his comments on POSH are in *Port Out, Starboard Home—And Other Language Myths*. The material quoted here comes from his entry on that word. I refer to Quinion in several other places.

Quinion explores several other possible explanations for the word's origin. "The most probable solution—although unprovable because slang is so rarely written down—is that it comes from London street slang for money."

In short, nobody knows for sure.

**

And there I was: previously satisfied that I had a handle on *posh* and its derivation. No, it wasn't much, just a bit of knowledge about one word—with literally hundreds of thousands of other English words that awaited conquest. Until now, though, I had a grasp on this *one* word and I was content. But then came the likes of Michael Quinion, who knew better and showed me my misplaced contentment about this word. Even worse, I was pushed into a new arena of insecurity and doubt. Was I wrong about other words or expressions?

Turns out I was. I had heard the saying, *cold enough to freeze the balls off a brass monkey*, which isn't as crude as it sounds. It referred to the cannon balls on a warship in the old days. They were stacked on a brass plate, called a monkey. But when it got cold enough the cannon balls would shrink and fall off the plate.

Quinion's evaluation of this account of the phrase's origin? "It's rubbish. There's no evidence that such brass plates existed."

My assumptions about etymology were challenged with spelling too. For example, I learned that *sacrilegious* wasn't based on the word *religion*, which explains why it wasn't spelled *sacriligious*. It is derived from *sacrilege*. Similarly, *minuscule* (a word I loved to include in tests for my students) was based on *minute*, as in extremely tiny—not mini- anything.

My newfound critical eye then extended to quotations. We all know that Edmund Burke said, "The only thing necessary for evil to triumph is for good men to do nothing." Not so. He may have expressed that sentiment, indirectly, but there's no record of him having used these words. Raining on Burke's parade are Paul F. Boller Jr and John George, in their book, *They Never Said It: A Book of Fake Quotes, Misquotes, and Misleading Attributions.*

Same with Mark Twain's famous aphorism, "Giving up smoking is easy. I've done it hundreds of times." Nope. No record of that in his writings. And what of his statement that "There are three kinds of lies: lies, damn lies, and statistics"? That's in his autobiography but he credits it to Benjamin Disraeli.

Or what of the hallowed words of George Gipp, the beloved Notre Dame footballer, to "Win one for the Gipper"? He supposedly told head coach Knute Rockne these words shortly before dying when he was a senior in college. Eight years later the Notre Dame team were up against Army. With the game tied 0-0 at half-time, Rockne inspired his team to go out and "Win one for the Gipper."[57] Well, they did. Final score: 12-6. This quote was one of President Ronald Reagan's favorites. As a sports broadcaster before entering acting and then politics, Reagan often quoted the young player's words. However, were they genuine? Here is Boller and George's assessment: "Probably not. Rockne was in the habit of thinking up all kinds of dramatic tales to inspire his players, and the Gipp story was almost certainly one of them. Reagan himself admitted that Rockne may have invented the tale, but he didn't think it mattered, because it inspired his team 'to sacrifice their individual quarrels for a common goal.'"

***

So, is nothing sacred? Well, when it comes to word origins and sourcing of quotes, it pays to take seriously something else President Reagan said, about arms treaties and the Russians: "Trust, but verify."[58]

---

[57] Then there's the spoof in the movie *Airplane* concerning George Zip, and the pitch to "Win one for the Zipper." But that's another story.

[58] Which, conveniently for Reagan's purposes, is a rhyming proverb in Russian. They would have understood.

Prepositions

Despite all the logic against it, some people persist in saying one shouldn't end a sentence with a preposition. Next time someone reprimands you for doing so, ask: *"What are you talking about?"*

Another possible response is to agree with the person, apologize for letting your standards slip, and lament the state of English in general. Then say, *"Yes, it's clear—the rot has set in."* Watch for the response.

***

A young boy was sent to bed on the promise that Mom would come upstairs and read him a story. But the book she chose was not his favorite and in response he asked her, *"What did you bring the book I didn't want to be read to out of up for?"*

But now, wait for it, supposedly the world record for the most prepositions ending a sentence: *"What did you turn your socks from inside in to inside out instead of from outside out to inside in for?"*

Problems with Worms

Ronnie Barker was one of Britain's greatest comedians in the twentieth century. His partnership with Ronnie Corbett led to a long running show titled, not surprisingly, *The Two Ronnies*. Many of their sketches hinged on word play and resulting misunderstanding. One of Barker's best-known series of sketches dealt with a society for people who struggled to pronounce their words. Here's the opening of one of those monologues.

> *Good evening. I am the president of the Loyal Society for the Relief of Suffers from Pismronunciation, for the relief of people who can't say their worms correctly, or who use the wrong worms entirely, so that other people cannot underhand a bird they are spraying. It's just that you open your mouse, and the worms come turbling out in wuck a say that you dick not what you're thugging to be, and it's very distressing.*

These sketches are readily available on YouTube and a perfect antidote to a wide range of maladies that can be cured by laughter.

Prophetic Words

Thanks to Paul Dickson's prodigious word-gathering efforts over the years, we have in his anthology *Dickson's Word Treasury* lists of words on the most obscure of topics—like the one he terms "Prophetic Words." Elsewhere we've referred to *tyromancy*, meaning how to foretell the future using cheese.[59] Dickson offers about another 160 of these predictive words. He doesn't say how extensively they've been used over the years but the fact that these terms exist suggests that someone, somewhere has tried or at least envisaged those particular methods of discerning the future. Nor does Dickson state the success rate of these approaches to divination. The words listed here, excerpted from his book, are for informational purposes only.[60] For your convenience, we are providing only approaches that can be tried in your home or office.

- *Alomancy*—Divining the future by means of salt.
- *Cartopedy*—By the lines on the soles of the feet.
- *Cleidomancy*—By a key hanging from a young girl's third fingernail.
- *Dririmancy*—By dripping blood.

---

[59] In the section on **Ten Words Beginning With the Letter T**.

[60] Disclaimer: Applying any of these words to discern the future is done expressly at the user's risk. The user agrees that he/she/pronoun of choice will not hold the author or Paul Dickson responsible for any damages or other undesirable outcome, including unexpectedly depressing forecasts of the future. No offer, either explicit or implicit, is made that any predictions of the future will turn out as the user's chosen method has predicted. Nor is there any warranty that such chosen method will yield any prediction in the first place.

- *Micromancy*—By the smallest thing at hand.
- *Nephelomancy*—By the clouds.
- *Odontomancy*—By examining teeth.
- *Oomancy*—By means of eggs, usually broken.
- *Retromancy*—By looking over one's shoulder.
- *Seyomancy*—By means of a cup.[61]

---

[61] Please be assured that bizarre though they may seem, these are all genuine words listed by Dickson.

Punctuation

While this is a book about words, the fact is: punctuation matters. Here's one example to prove the point that how you separate words with these funny little marks makes a world of difference: Note the difference between "Let's eat, Grandma" and "Let's eat Grandma."

Then, if you get men and women to punctuate the following, you may well get two different results: "Woman without her man is a savage."

- Men may likely say, "Woman, without her man, is a savage."
- Women are more likely to go with, "Woman! Without her, man is a savage."

One more example. When Richard Brinsley Sheridan was a Member of Parliament in England he was once required to apologize for using unparliamentary language. He had called a fellow member a liar. He complied with the order from the Speaker of the House as follows: "Mr. Speaker: I said the honorable member was a liar it is true and I am sorry for it." Then he added that the honorable member could punctuate the sentence as he pleased.

Puns

A pun has been described as the lowest form of wit—unless you thought of it first. Regardless of their merits, they'll be with us in perpetuity; we cannot resist their playfulness and cleverness. At least, some of us can't.

This section includes only puns attributed to real people. The Internet offers hundreds of fabricated puns, marked by varying degrees of sophistication and humor, some appealing to children from 3 or 4 years on up. As children begin to delight in the playful opportunities that language offers, they revel in telling their parents and friends things like:

- *Humpty Dumpty had a terrible summer but then had a great fall,* or
- *The duck said to the shopkeeper, "Just put it on my bill."*

Hilaire Belloc
This English author wrote his own witty epitaph:

When I am dead, I hope it may be said:
"His sins were scarlet, but his books were read."

Michael Berman
The only non-famous name in this list, Michael was a classmate of mine at Sea Point Boys' High, in Cape Town. I am including him here because he delivered one of the timeliest puns I have ever heard, one that I recall vividly and with admiration near sixty years later.

We were in an English class when our substitute teacher was taking us through a poem, "Smuggler's Leap," by the English poet Richard Barham. It was a long poem and we grew restless, despite the teacher's dramatic reading. Then he came to the critical moment, the climax of the poem when the horse (a dun) had disappeared: "But where was that dun, that terrible dun?"

Michael delivered the answer, with impeccable timing: "Dunno...." The class collapsed in uncontrollable laughter for who knows how many minutes.

I don't recall how long the substitute teacher was with us after that.

John Donne

This sixteenth century poet and clergyman wrote in "A Hymn to God the Father": "But swear by thyself that at my death thy Son / Shall shine as he shines now, and heretofore;/ And, having done that, thou hast done; / I fear no more."

Mental Floss includes this passage in its list of fifteen of history's greatest puns. It says that "There's a lot going on here, and you need a bit more information to fully unpack this pun from 'A Hymn to God the Father'.... While the play on son/sun and corresponding reference to 'shining' are fairly obvious, the real kicker is Donne's allusion to himself and his wife, Anne Moore, in the final lines ('thou has *done*; I fear no *more*')."

Ben Franklin

This pun, attributed to one of the Founding Fathers, Ben Franklin, also made *Mental Floss'* top-fifteen list. Committing to the revolution against Britain was a treasonous offence, which led to this comment: "We must all hang together or assuredly we shall all hang separately."

Groucho Marx

Groucho was a member of the famous Marx brothers group, known for their crazy antics in a series of movies in the 1930s and 1940s. Wikipedia says, "They are widely considered by critics, scholars, and fans to be among the greatest and most influential comedians of the twentieth century." Groucho was best known and he went on to a successful television career after the troupe disbanded. On one occasion he was in a restaurant when his former wife showed up. His comment: "Marx spots the Ex."

Dorothy Parker

The wit and writer Dorothy Parker was apparently asked if she could make a pun on the word "horticulture." Her response: "You can lead a horticulture but you can't make her think."

Peccavi

The British general, Sir Charles Napier, is credited with a brilliant bilingual pun. Upon establishing military control[62] over the province of Sind, now part of Pakistan, Napier sent a one-word telegram to his superiors: "Peccavi." That is Latin for "I have sinned."

However, the truth is that Napier never sent that message. It was made up by a teenager, Catherine Winkworth, who submitted the pun to a humor magazine. It was then mistakenly attributed to the general's brilliance. Winkworth grew up to become a prolific writer and translator of dozens of hymns and is perhaps best known for "Now Thank We All Our God."

A Joke: The Florist

A florist who had sold out of flowers and had only ferns available, said to a man wanting a bouquet: "With fronds like these, who needs anenomes?"

***

And finally, "A good pun is its own reword."

---

[62] Expressly against the orders he had received, incidentally.

Puns—A Bonus

Many puns are contrived and far from spontaneous. Nevertheless, some of them are to be admired for their cleverness. One example is of the Texan who handed over his beef cattle ranch to his three sons and renamed the estate "Focus." He explained that this was now "The place where the sons raise meat."[63]

Deserving special mention are two British radio personalities, Frank Muir and Denis Norden. They were in their heyday in the 1950s and 1960s, and were known throughout the English-speaking British Commonwealth countries for their radio comedy. Among their accomplishments was a radio game show titled *My Word*. The culminating feature of each week's show involved Muir and Norden getting a well-known phrase or a line from literature. Their task was to explain its origin, which they did through witty, imaginative and totally fabricated stories—all of which ended with a tortured punning version of their assigned line. Among their versions, and the originals, were:

- *Karate begins a tome (Charity begins at home.)*
- *Now is the time for Lord Goodman to come to the aid of the potty. (Now is the time for all good men to come to the aid of the party.)*
- *You can't have your kayak and heat it. (You can't have your cake and eat it.)*

Their stories are highly entertaining and it's worth buying a compilation from an on-line bookstore.

---

[63] Or, "The place where the sun's rays meet."

Repartee

Some people have a gift for a swift and ingeniously appropriate response to a provocative situation, leaving us astonished at how some minds can combine these two qualities with such effectiveness. The example that follows, like many memorable exchanges, is attributed to a number of British notables. But the authoritative quoteinvestigator.com website says the most likely participants were Samuel Foote, a dramatist and comedic actor, and Lord Sandwich. Here's the website's account of Foote's arrival at a social gathering:

> When the Comedian entered, the Peer exclaimed, "What, are you alive still?" "Yes, my Lord," replied Foote. "Pray Sam," retorted his Lordship, "which do you think will happen to you first, the experience of a certain disease, or an intimate acquaintance with the gallows?" "Why," rejoined the Comedian, "that depends upon circumstances, and they are these, whether I prefer embracing your Lordship's mistress, or your principles."

***

Winston Churchill and playwright George Bernard Shaw, both giants in their respective arenas, apparently had this exchange over the opening of one of Shaw's plays:

Shaw: "I am reserving two tickets for you for my premier. Come and bring a friend—if you have one."

Churchill: "Impossible to be present for the first performance. Will attend the second—if there is one."

***

One more example of a politician's wit came from down under. Australian Prime Minister Robert Menzies was heckled at a campaign event when a woman shouted, "I wouldn't vote for you if you were the Archangel Gabriel."

Menzies: "If I were the Archangel Gabriel, madam, you would not be in my constituency."

***

Nor are razor sharp responses limited to adults. Playwright and critic George Kaufman, aged 4, responding to his mother when she said that his aunt was coming to visit. She said: "It wouldn't hurt to be nice to her, would it?" He said: "That depends on your threshold of pain."

***

The brilliant writer Dorothy Parker was famous for her work on *The New Yorker* magazine but also for her sharp retorts. Here are three examples.

- *The New Yorker* initially struggled financially and on one occasion its editor, Harold Ross, noticed Parker downstairs in a coffee shop. He asked what she was doing there when she should have been working upstairs in the magazine's offices. She said, "Someone else is using the pencil."
- Parker did not get on with Clare Booth Luce, the wife of *Time* magazine founder Henry Luce and a highly able woman herself. She was a member of Congress, an author, and the first woman appointed to a major ambassadorial position. On one occasion they were approaching an entrance wide enough for only one of them. Luce gestured for Parker to go ahead, saying, "Age before beauty." Parker stepped ahead, with the comment: "Pearls before swine."

- On being told that the taciturn President Calvin Coolidge had died, she asked, "How can they tell?"

***

Fittingly, we'll give Coolidge himself the last word. Known for his extremely non-conversational ways, he was once approached by a person at a gathering, who said he had taken a bet that he could get Coolidge to say at least three words in conversation. Coolidge's reply: "You lose."

The *Right* Word

This entry overlaps with others, especially **Errors Lists**, **Pet Peeves** and **Tricky Words**. Steven Pinker, in *The Sense of Style*, provides two lists of problem words or phrases. The first he describes as "a few fuss-budget decrees you can safely ignore...." He bases these choices on "data from the AHD [*American Heritage Dictionary of the English Language*] Usage Panel, historical analyses from several dictionaries, and a pinch of my own judgment." His first word here is *Aggravate*—and that's where he and I have our first disagreement. He is far more relaxed than I am about accepting the word as having the sense of "annoy," rather than "worsen an existing condition." I concede that he's on solid ground. He notes that the sense of "annoy" has been in use since the seventeenth century and is accepted by 83 percent of the AHD Usage Panel. Still, I think there's a useful distinction here.

His second list consists of words or phrases whose distinct meanings he thinks are worth preserving. Unlike his fuss-budget list, the second one, he says, "is a list of words which I am prepared to try to dissuade you from using in their nonstandard senses."

Whether you know it or not, or whether you've thought about it or not, you also have these two lists: the words whose more casual or popular meaning is OK with you, and those where you draw the line and say, "Wait a minute, you're using X the wrong way. Let me set you straight." (At least, we'll think this even if we don't say it aloud.)

Each of us also thinks our two lists are sensible, valid and defensible, and therefore everyone else's is flawed. Admittedly, the "OK/Not OK" lists of a linguist of Steven Pinker's standing carry far more weight in the public arena than mine. My lists overlap considerably with his, and perhaps with yours as well. But they won't be identical. The uniqueness of everyone's lists speaks to the slipperiness of trying to establish uniform usage standards in our speech and writing. Some of us, for instance, will even justify using *irregardless*. Even though Pinker and other authorities point us to what's considered "nonstandard" and "standard," in the end we all devise our own lists of what we regard as the right words.

And despite the evidence he presents, I still think Pinker's wrong about *aggravate*, so I'll place this one atop my list of Right Words just to annoy (and I mean "annoy") him and those who agree with him.

***

Aggravate vs Annoy—*Annoy* means to irritate. *Aggravate* means to worsen an existing condition.

***

Bi- vs Semi—Pop quiz: What does *biweekly* mean: (1) twice a week, (2) every two weeks, (3) every alternate week? Two issues arise here. One is the meaning of these two prefixes. Bi- means "two" so *biweekly* means every two weeks. A bicentennial is every two hundred years. Semi-, by contrast, means "half," so semi-weekly means twice a week. So far so good (we hope). But here's the second issue. It is not enough for you to know the difference, it is crucial that your reader or listener understands your meaning. Because there's so much fuzziness surrounding these two prefixes, you're probably better off saying "twice a week" or whatever you mean.

***

Enormous or Enormousness vs Enormity—The first is something big, exceptionally big. The second is a less familiar word, with a distinctive meaning not related to size. It means something outrageous or monstrous. "The *enormity* of the Rwandan genocide shocked the world."

***

Ensure vs Insure—*Ensure* is to make sure something happens. "Mom will *ensure* I brush my teeth tonight." *Insure* is what you do for your car, your house, or your life.

***

Fulsome—This is related to being full but not in a way many people assume. *Fulsome* has strong negative connotations, such as "too much" or "over the top." *The Chicago Manual of Style's* section on word usage says the word connotes "excessive to the point of being repulsive."

***

Hang/Hanged/Hung—*The Chicago Manual of Style* is especially helpful here: "*Hanged* is used as the past participle of *hang* only in its transitive form when referring to the killing (just or unjust) of a human being by suspending the person by the neck (criminals were hanged at Tyburn Hill). But if death is not intended or likely, or if the person is suspended by a body part other than the neck, hung is correct (he was hung upside down as a cruel prank). In most senses, of course, *hung* is the past form of hang (Mark hung up his clothes). All inanimate objects, such as pictures and Christmas stockings, are hung."

***

Noisome—This word has nothing to do with noise. It means noxious or foul-smelling.

***

Ordinance vs Ordnance—The first is a law or rule instituted by a city government or similar body, the second is military things that go bang.

***

Tortuous vs Torturous—Both entail difficulty but in different ways. The first refers to twisting or winding conditions, as in "He drove too fast for my comfort on the tortuous road through the Alps." The second, thanks to the process of elimination, you have probably correctly concluded refers to *torture*.

Rhyme Time

The four most common non-rhyming words in English are *orange, silver, purple* and *month*. You won't find what we could call "naturally occurring" examples of any rhymes. But that hasn't stopped people from trying. Michael Quinion, an English word maven, cites the example of how Robert Browning managed to rhyme *month* and *orange*[64]—well, sort of—in this piece of doggerel:

From the Ganges to the Blorenge
Comes the Rajah once a month.
Sometimes chewing on an orange.
Sometimes reading from his Grunth.

Quinion says that Browning wasn't cheating by inventing words, noting that *Blorenge* is a small mountain in Wales, while *Grunth* is a Sikh holy book.

Other words that are notoriously difficult to rhyme are *lemon, penguin* and *silver*. Those who have succeeded had to engage in contortions or obscurities as bad as or even worse than Browning's.

Any other takers?

---

[64] We should note that the Oxford dictionary cites "sporange" as a rhyme for orange. It's an uncommon botanical term for a part of a fern. This is so obscure that I hardly think that counts. Agreed?

The Russell Conjugation

The English philosopher, Bertrand Russell, was on a BBC radio program and was asked to give an example of conjugating an irregular verb. He said, "I am firm. You are obstinate. He is a pig-headed fool." He was describing the same behavior but with varying levels of empathy toward each person:

- I am firm. [Positive empathy]
- You are obstinate. [Neutral to mildly negative empathy]
- He/She/It is pigheaded. [Very negative empathy]

Eric Weinstein, a mathematician and economist, says that "most words and phrases are actually defined not by a single dictionary description, but rather two distinct attributes: the factual content of the word or phrase, [and] the emotional content of the construction."

So it is that we can have words with the same factual content but with significantly different emotional implications. For example, we might call someone who spilled the beans about corruption in the mayor's office a *whistle-blower*. That is, unless we were the mayor, in which case he'd be a *snitch* or a *tattletale*. Similarly, Weinstein says, people in a focus group will oppose the idea of a *death tax* whereas moments before they favored an *estate tax,* exactly the same thing.

Following Russell's initial example on the radio, the *New Statesman* ran one of its famous competitions seeking additional examples. They got some 2,000 responses. Other publications have repeated the exercise, yielding a rich array of results. Drawing on several of these sources, I herewith present you this sampling:

- I have reconsidered it. You have changed your mind. He has gone back on his word.
- I am righteously indignant. You are annoyed. He is making a fuss over nothing.
- I enjoy a tipple. You drink too much. He is a soak.
- I am beautiful. You are pretty. She has a good personality.
- I am descended from the earliest settlers of this town. You are a local girl. She is the product of centuries of in-breeding.

**

Think of other ways we use words that end up reinforcing our own opinions or ideas. For example, we regard those rebels on the border as terrorists. That is, until they overthrow the evil regime, when they are transformed into the freedom fighters who secured our liberty. We could construct another conjugation: I am a freedom fighter. You are a guerilla. He is a terrorist.

Well, time to move on. I have said just the right amount on this topic. You would prefer more. He is impossible to please.

Scrabble

Gyles Brandreth once got a phone call at 4 a.m. from an anxious Scrabble player who wanted to know if the word *yex* is allowed. As Brandreth writes in his book, *The Joy of Lex*, the answer is yes. It's an archaic word meaning a hiccup—but acceptable in play. The occasion for the call was the first British Scrabble Championship, which he had launched. The player was competing to reach the finals.

Scrabble players, you will soon learn if you rub shoulders with them, take the game *very, very* seriously.[65] It is the ultimate word game, having been on the scene in one form or another in the United States since 1938. It has sold about 150 million copies. It is estimated that a third of US homes and a half of British homes have a set. Scrabble players have tournaments, their own dictionary, and rigorous rules about playing the game (beyond what you will find in the box). About 4,000 Scrabble clubs have formed around the world. The game is the subject of documentaries and has been modified into a TV game show in the United States.

While Scrabble clearly overshadows the word games market, the keen word-gamer has plenty of other choices. See **Word Games**.

---

[65] In the section on **Weak Words** I sneer at the word "very." In this instance, however, a double-very is entirely justified.

Shakespeare

Shakespeare's genius wasn't only as a dramatist and poet; he was a wordsmith par excellence. When he could not find the words he needed, he made them up. He is credited with coining not dozens, nor hundreds, but nearly 2,000 of them. The Shakespeare Birthplace Trust says he "likely invented or introduced at least 1,700 words into the English language. He did this by combining words, changing nouns into verbs, adding prefixes or suffixes, and so on. Some words stayed and some didn't." The organization notes that lexicographers keep finding new examples of Shakespeare's bold originality.

This was a daring strategy for a playwright whose business consisted of connecting immediately with an audience. You have to be pretty bold and confident that the words you're inventing will be grasped immediately by your hearers. Many of the words, as already noted, are built on existing forms. But to introduce so many words that are now part of our everyday vocabularies is a feat no other writer has even remotely matched. But then, he was Shakespeare....

Here are ten words from the Shakespeare Birthplace Trust's lists of A-Z contributions:

1. *Alligator*
2. *Bedroom*
3. *Critic*
4. *Downstairs*
5. *Eyeball*
6. *Fashionable*
7. *Gossip*
8. *Hurry*

9. Inaudible
10.Jaded
11.Kissing

We cheated; we gave you eleven instead. How could we possibly omit the last one? And that raises the question, What did people before Shakespeare's time call this practice (which we can safely assume didn't come into existence only with the Bard's naming it)?[66]

The full list ends in *zany*, which for the record comes from *Love's Labour's Lost*, Act 5 Scene 2.[67] The full list is well worth checking out on the Trust's website.

---

[66] Probably not *osculation*.

[67] This example is a bit of stretch, in that zany is used in this play as a noun, not as an adjective—which is the customary contemporary usage. The website says it means a "clown's assistant; performer who mimics another's antics."

Shibboleth

Wikipedia defines a shibboleth as "any custom or tradition, usually a choice of phrasing or even a single word, that distinguishes one group of people from another." For example, if you grew up speaking British English you're likely to pronounce the word *schedule* as *shedule*. Most Americans are likely to say *skedule*. However, this wouldn't be a true shibboleth, as one can easily adjust one's pronunciation. A true shibboleth is like the one referred to in the book of Judges in the Bible.

The Gileadites routed the Ephraimites and captured the fords of the Jordan leading to Ephraim. When a surviving Ephraimite tried to make it home, he was asked if he was from Ephraim. If he said "no," then came the test: "Say the word 'Shibboleth,'" a Hebrew word meaning the part of a plant containing grain. "If he said, 'Sibboleth,' because he could not pronounce the word correctly, they seized him and killed him at the fords of the Jordan." (Judges 12:6)

During World War II American forces in the Pacific used the word "lollapalooza" as a test for a suspected Japanese infiltrator; a Japanese spy or potential attacker would most likely pronounce the L's as R's.

More recently, US border officials used the alphabet to test people crossing the US-Canadian border during the Vietnam war. Many young Americans fled to Canada to avoid the draft and then wanted to return for a visit, or perhaps permanently. If they claimed they were Canadian, they would pronounce the last letter of the alphabet as "zed." Anyone who said "zee" gave away his true American upbringing and was in serious trouble, although not quite of Ephraimite proportions.

More innocent ways shibboleths emerge concern what may seem as quirky pronunciations of local names. Anyone in my city, Spokane, who pronounces it as "spo-KANE" is a dead give-away as an outsider; we all know better and call it "spo-KAN." Going a little farther afield, there's the episode in our family's visit to Ireland. We needed directions to Dun Laoghaire, just outside Dublin. But referring to it as "Dun Log-hair"—a logical best guess, I thought—brought helpful instructions and a correction: it's "Dun Leery."

Then, in case you're ever going to need to prove you're authentically Czech or Slovak, be prepared to say *strč prst skrz krk*, a tongue twister meaning "stick a finger through the throat." It is especially difficult for a non-native speaker because of the absence of vowels. (It sounds pretty much impossible even for a native speaker.)

Short Words

I am a bear of Very Little Brain and long words bother me.
   —Winnie the Pooh

One of the most difficult lessons to instill in college students is that long, polysyllabic words are not nearly as dazzling for their professors as they might think. They will have to learn some fancy schmancy words as part of the specialized discipline in which they major. But especially in writing classes it is difficult to get them to embrace short words and short sentences.

Time to introduce them to examples like the 1938 essay, "Short Words Are Words of Might," by Gelett Burgess, a critic and author. What's noteworthy about this sixteen-page essay is that it is written entirely with words of one syllable. Here's a short excerpt:

> *Short words must have been our first words when the world was young. The minds of men were raw…. Their first words were, no doubt, mere grunts or growls, barks, whines, squeals like those of beasts. These rough, strange sounds were made to show how they felt. They meant joy or pain or doubt or rage or fear…. Short words, you see, come from down deep in us—from our hearts or guts—not from the brain. For they deal for the most part with things that move and sway us, that make us act… That, I think, is why short words tend to make our thoughts more live and true.*

***

Now an exercise. Find the last three pieces of writing you've done, preferably saved on your computer. For each piece, count the total number of words. Then see how many of those are words of more than one syllable. There's nothing wrong with longer words, if they are the *right* words. Now, take the piece with the largest proportion of longer words and ask yourself, how much would it please or bother Winnie the Pooh?

Signs

It all began with the discovery of a book on a clearance table outside a New York bookstore. It was titled *Jail Keys Made Here—And Other Signs*. I bought it immediately. The photographed signs included such gems as "Stereo Tapes for People with Two Ears," "Special Broken Pies 5¢ Each," and the "Co-Existence Bagel Shop."

That was in the mid-1970s. I was immediately hooked and so began my journey of noticing signs in a new way and photographing them. Eventually I had enough to put on a presentation which I linked to my South African background. I would ask audiences to imagine I was a newcomer to the United States and was faced with this bewildering array of messages. I put together a slide show (this was in the pre-PowerPoint era) and would tell my audiences my three rules for interpreting the signs.

- If I could possibly misinterpret a sign, I would.
- I would normally not reveal the context of a sign, and
- I did not tamper with signs; what I saw on a reader-board, for example, is what I photographed.

What intrigued me about signs, like **Headlines**, is that they have to convey a message in an extremely confined space. This means that, also like headlines, the pressure of getting a message in print can easily result in inadvertently overlooking clarity or even common sense, which leads one to ask, "What *were* they getting at?" That explains why my collection includes the following:

- Entrance Only—Do Not Enter.
- Cemetery—No Dumping.
- Do It Yourself—We Can Help!
- Dead End Residents Only.
- Ladies Pants—Half Off.
- Non-accessible entrance.
- No Parking on Railroad Tracks Except When Train is Coming.

***

Others were included because they are unusual or lend themselves to the kind of perverse and deliberate misinterpretation that I enjoy:

- Extreme Caution When Flashing.[68]
- Use Right Shoulder to Install Chains.
- Brentwood Elementary School: Activity Day—Parent Barbecue.
- Do Not Force Head Into Diving Helmet.
- Road Closed—Jesuit Cars Only.

***

I conclude the presentation with a badly rusting sign that's showing its age: Disregard This Sign.[69] Clearly, someone has.

---

[68] Generally a good principle in life, I would argue.
[69] Obviously a spoof but still worth including.

Spelling

He respects Owl, because you can't help respecting anybody who can spell Tuesday, even if he doesn't spell it right.
— *A. A. Milne*

Try this test on any friend who claims to be a good speller: "Outside a cemetery stood a harassed beggar and an embarrassed peddler gauging the symmetry of the new skyscraper with unparalleled ecstasy."

Ten Commonly Misspelled Words

- *Accommodate*
- *Consensus*
- *Definitely*—This one often is transformed by spellcheck into *defiantly*, as in "I will *defiantly* be at your grandma's funeral."
- *Inoculate*
- *Liaison*
- *Minuscule*—This word is based on *minute*.
- *Occurred*
- *Receive*—A useful spelling rule for those tricky -IE- and -EI- words is LICE; it doesn't always work but it does in many settings, such as bel<u>ie</u>ve, dec<u>ei</u>ve, rel<u>ie</u>ve.
- *Sacrilegious*—This word is based on "sacrilege," with *-lege*, not "religious," with *relig-*.
- *Separate*

***

Next time you misspell a word see it as an opportunity to make that the *last* time you do so. How? Two suggestions: One is to remember the root of the word, as with *minuscule* and *sacrilegious*. Another is by devising some mind-game or word picture to help you remember the tricky part of the word. Often it's a matter of whether you need one letter or two. So, with *accommodate*, for example, you could imagine a motel that has a "No Vacancies" sign outside, indicating that there's no room for any more people... or letters; it's already full with the two Cs and the two Ms. With *inoculate*, the issue is "one N or two?" Imagine the N stands for a needle. As for me, one needle (and one N) is enough if I am getting an inoculation. Problem solved.

Spellcheck—And The Cupertino Effect

Spellcheck is an invaluable tool for catching your misspellings and innocent typos. So, spellcheck is fine, insofar as it goes.

But beware of the Cupertino effect. First, some background. Cupertino is a town in California, which happens to be the headquarters of Apple. And the name could well make its way into your writing in error if you're using an older version of a spell checker and you're not paying attention. If you typed *cooperation* and your spell checker knew only *co-operation*, it might insert Cupertino as the suggested correction. Embarrassing examples of this problem came from the European Central Bank, which asked in a document, "Could you tell us how far such policy can go under the euro zone, and specifically where the limits of this Cupertino would be?"

A United Nations report argued for "improving the efficiency of international Cupertino." And a good thing too, you might say.

Other amusing examples have included *Voldemort* from Harry Potter being replaced with *Voltmeter* and the *Muttahida Qaumi Movement*, a Pakistani political party, appearing in print as the *Muttonhead Quail Movement*.

As the *New Scientist* magazine noted, "If you have ever received a document containing off-putting expressions such as 'At your desecration' or 'Sorry for the incontinence,' then you have witnessed the havoc that can be wreaked by placing unthinking trust in spellcheckers."

Spoonerisms

Nobody would put the Rev. William Archibald Spooner in the same category as Sam Goldwyn. (See **Goldwynisms**.) Assuming you've read this book's entries sequentially, you now know that Sam Goldwyn was the movie mogul to whom a wide range of amusing sayings were attributed. Spooner lived in a different world. He was a cleric and an academic, who was a scholar at Oxford University's New College[70] from 1862 to 1924.

Their lives found common ground, however, in that Spooner also served as a trigger for countless sayings that were attributed to him but which, as with Goldwyn, he never said. Known as Spoonerisms, these muddled expressions had a basis in fact. Spooner was known to get things mixed up. The World Wide Words website[71] says examples that are regarded as authentic include a reference to a friend of a certain Dr. Child as "Dr. Friend's child." Another was the occasion when he and a companion passed by a woman dressed in black. Spooner commented that the woman's "late husband was a very sad case, poor man, 'eaten by missionaries.'" His behavior too included backwards actions, like the time at a college dinner when he spilled some salt and then poured claret on it to mop it up, just the opposite of normal procedure.

Still, the World Wide Words article says, "Virtually every example on record, including all the famous ones, is an invention by ingenious members of the university, who, as one undergraduate remembers, used to spend hours making them up."

---

[70] "New College" is a relative concept: it was founded in 1379.
[71] http://www.worldwidewords.org/qa/qa-spo4.htm.

We must therefore give credit to these well-known Spoonerisms to unknown wordsmiths.

- "Young man, you have hissed my mystery lectures and tasted your worm and you must leave Oxford by the town drain." (In case you're reading this late at night and need help with the translation, it is "Young man, you have missed my history lectures and wasted your term and you must leave Oxford by the train down.")
- "Let us raise our glasses to the queer old dean."

The World Wide Words piece concludes, "Spooner was an excellent lecturer, speaker and administrator who did much to transform New College into a modern institution. But he was no great scholar, and it's a cruel twist of fate that he is now only remembered for a concept he largely had foisted on him."

.

Style

When it comes to words, we can think of style in two senses. One is an individual writer's particular approach to his or her craft. What makes Ernest Hemingway or James Joyce distinctive as story tellers? Or Stephen King or Danielle Steel? That's not our focus here, however. We will look only at style in the sense of a consistent approach to written material. For example, if you were writing a research paper on the former Libyan ruler, would you refer to him as:

1. Moammar Gaddafi
2. Muammar al-Gaddafi
3. Moammar Kadafi
4. Moammar Gadhafi
5. Muammar el-Qaddafi

Here's how various news organizations deal with that question. The Associated Press, CNN, and MSNBC go with no. 4. *The New York Times* goes with no. 5. The *Los Angeles Times* opts for no. 3. Reuters, *The Guardian*, and the BBC settled on no. 2. *The Irish Times* goes with none of the above, preferring "Muammar Gadafy." And *The Christian Science Monitor*, which did a story on the variants of the man's names, committed to yet another option: "Muammar Qaddafi."

ABC News, which uses option 1 above, has compiled "a list of 112 variations on the English spellings of the former Libyan strongman's name," the *Monitor* reported.

***

This is an extreme case, resulting from two factors. One is that there are no easy ways to settle on English spellings of Arabic names. The other is that the man never indicated what his preferred English spelling should be, which is usually the standard that news media and other style-conscious organizations adopt. But the Gaddafi example[72] makes a crucial point. While none of these options is right or wrong, a writer or an editor has to settle on something, and then stick with it. You can't have Gaddafi on page 1 and Qaddafi on page 2. Alert readers will pick this up and you'd look stupid.

Any book or magazine editor wants to receive a manuscript marked by consistency and adherence to a preferred style manual. What do you do in your treatment of numbers, for example? If you're following Associated Press style, in general you will spell out numbers up to nine and from 10 onwards they'll be figures. For example, you'll have "I ate nine hotdogs and 10 donuts." Exceptions: Ages are always figures. So are city council, Supreme Court or similar votes: "A 5-4 decision."

Wait? Did I just cite *The Associated Press Stylebook*? Sorry. I meant to say *The Chicago Manual of Style*. That's the law for almost all US book publishers. And the CMS[73] has its own rules. For example, it requires most numbers to be spelled out up to one hundred, unlike the AP's cut-off at 10.... Sorry, ten.

---

[72] Oh, what the heck—let's just go with no. 1.
[73] Most likely a futile attempt to impress a prospective publisher for this book with knowledge of trade terminology.

Taboo Words

In 1992 I was studying Spanish in Guatemala. I participated in an intensive immersion program that included a home stay with a kind couple, Lucy and Gustavo. They were wonderfully patient and forgiving as I barbarized their language. One evening over dinner I was speaking when each of them broke into a grin. Gustavo then told me I had said "a bad word." It was obviously bad enough that they refused to tell me what I had, in all innocence, brought to the evening meal. Knowing the context, that I had said the word unwittingly, they realized there was nothing to forgive and the matter was closed.

That's not always the case, however, as the late comedian George Carlin learned following a radio broadcast of his now famous "Seven Dirty Words" monologue. It had to do with a broadcast at 2 in the afternoon. The time was significant because the person who complained, and triggered a series of court cases that culminated with a 1978 US Supreme Court decision, was with his 15-year-old son at the time and heard the broadcast on a car radio. The father said this material should not have been aired when children were more likely to be listening, but rather late at night.

The outcome of the case and how the Federal Communications Commission can regulate indecent speech (and define it in the first place) is too detailed to examine here. Google it if you want to know more. Nor will we list Carlin's words here. The point of this example, though, is to show that societies struggle over what is acceptable speech, and under what circumstances certain words may be permitted—if at all.

A quick look at the derivation of *taboo* is useful. It was introduced into English by Captain Cook, who encountered it in Polynesia on his third voyage around the world. It is a Tongan word, *tapu*, meaning prohibited or sacred. Cook noticed how certain behaviors in that society were strictly avoided, a "taboo"—a concept that we now apply to anything that we regard as off limits.

The acceptability of taboo words varies over time. It's now laughable to us that in Victorian times it was unacceptable to refer to *trousers*. Instead, *nether garments* was the **Euphemism** you needed. Any mention of *legs* was also a no-no; you needed to say *limbs*. Given this era's prudish approach to anything having to do with sex, the word *pregnant* also had to be replaced with phrases like *to be expecting* or *to be with child*.

***

It is important to note that taboo words attain that status because enough people in a society define them as bad or objectionable words. There is nothing inherent in a word itself that causes a problem, as linguists will tell you; it's the meaning we accord it, and with taboo words, the baggage that comes along with it.

What types of words become taboo in polite society? We can identify at least six categories.

- "Dirty" words, having to do with sex or excretion.[74]
- Parts of the body (especially what the Monty Python people would term the "naughty bits").
- Racial or ethnic slurs.
- Personal insults.
- Sacred things.
- Hate speech.

---

[74] For a comprehensive anthology of taboo words see Hugh Rawson: *Wicked Words*. Two others dealing with taboo words are Benjamin Bergen: *What the F: What Swearing Reveals About Our Language* and Emma Byrne's *Swearing is Good for You*.

Of course, in each category it is the person hearing or reading the word who decides if it falls in a taboo category or not. So it may be acceptable for one African American to call another a *nigger* in a jocular or friendly way; it is a major taboo in the contemporary United States for a white person to do so. You will have noticed that this six-fold list overlaps with **Political Correctness**.

The ideal is that we avoid these studiously in polite society or if we are seeking to avoid a confrontation. Perhaps we resort to them when we are angry, feel strongly in making a point, or have just jammed our finger in a car door. Or depending on our circle of friends, we may draw on one or more of these six categories in casual conversation. With our friends, we may even delight in violating these taboos. Settings are also a key determinant on how free we feel to use taboo words. A construction site foreman will be more tolerant of violations than a teacher in an elementary school classroom.

Now and again people who are expected to avoid using taboo words get caught out, as Richard Nixon learned when his secret tapes entered the public realm. People got to see a different side of the man. Just as I, for a fleeting moment, was in danger of being redefined by Lucy and Gustavo.

Tact

Tact is the art of making a point without making an enemy.
   —Isaac Newton

Tact fails as soon as it's noticed.
   —Unknown

You can learn everything you need to know about tact by observing the British TV show, *Doc Martin*. Martin Clunes plays the leading character, a doctor in a small Cornish village who is a brilliant medical practitioner but is also embarrassingly blunt, insensitive and utterly tactless. Study carefully Doc Martin's choice of words as he interacts with people; then do exactly the opposite.

His fundamental flaw is that his speech is totally devoid of empathy, the core of tactful speech. He seems unable to imagine how his patients will respond to negative news about a diagnosis or a firm admonition to cut out unhealthy habits. Kind and gentle he is not.

In case you don't have immediate access to the Doc Martin programs or can't afford the time to make a study of his tactlessness, consider these seven principles.

- Remind yourself of the power of words to upset or hurt people, especially when needing to deliver bad news. Imagine how you would feel if you were on the receiving end of the message you're about to deliver. Consider rehearsing what you will say if you're facing a particularly awkward situation, like firing someone. Are your words likely to be received as patronizing, demeaning, or in some other way hurtful? This may be just the occasion when using **Euphemisms** is warranted.

- Prepare people for an unwelcome message. Preface your remarks by saying something like, "Celia, I'm afraid I have some bad news for you about the Jeep. You know how I said there were several possible causes of the oil leak. Well, I'm afraid it's the head gasket. This is a complicated repair on your particular model..." Better that than blurting out, "Hi Celia, we're looking at about $4,000 to fix this sucker."

- Do what you can to minimize a person's embarrassment. Let's say you're at a business gathering and you notice your boss has forgotten to do up his fly. You can go up to him while he's chatting and tell him directly and humiliate him in front of others. Or you can ask him to step aside as you have something important to tell him. Another alternative is to slip him a note that says, "Check your zip."

- Remember that tactfulness is all about the other person's wellbeing, not yours. You want to spare him or her pain, embarrassment, or some other negative experience.

- If the situation permits, ask if there is a creative solution that will address your concern without inflicting needless hurt on the other person. For example, a diplomat at a high-end dinner function noticed that a guest was surreptitiously sneaking expensive silver cutlery into her purse. He hid some knives and forks inside his jacket and approached the woman. Drawing her aside, he said conspiratorially as he showed her his own collection of silverware, "I'm afraid we've both been spotted; we're going to have to put these back." It worked and with less embarrassment for the thief than a direct confrontation.

- Look for whatever positive responses you can give, even if your inclination is to be negative. Someone gives you a birthday gift that you think is hideous. You can of course tell the person that this is the ugliest sweater you've ever seen and cannot imagine being seen wearing it in public. Or you can focus instead on this person's kindness: "I'm touched that you thought of me."

- Shut up. At times the most tactful course is to say nothing. I once visited a used bookstore in a small town where some of my relatives lived. I found on the shelves one of my books, which I had given these relatives several years before; the personalized inscription made that clear. I toyed with the idea of buying the book and giving it to them once again. But the tactful thing was to do, and say, nothing.

***

Let's finish with two more examples of tactful responses that spared a monarch embarrassment, and possibly the careers of those who said them. The first is from France. Louis XIV had a greatly inflated opinion of his skills as a poet. He once asked one of his courtiers, Nicolas Boileau, who was himself a highly accomplished poet, to read some of his work. Boileau managed to extricate himself from his difficult situation, and not humiliate his monarch, by saying, "Sire, nothing is impossible for your majesty. Your majesty has set out to write bad verses and has succeeded."

Next is the Duke of Wellington, the mastermind behind England's defeat of France at Waterloo. King George IV became more and more convinced that he had taken part in that battle when he hadn't even been present. After yet another recital about his imagined accomplishments on that battlefield, he turned to Wellington and asked, "Was it not so, duke?" Wellington replied: "I have often heard your majesty say so."[75]

***

See also **Kind Words**

---

[75] Both these anecdotes are from *The Little Brown Book of Anecdotes,* ed. Clifton Fadiman.

Ten Words Beginning the with Letter T[76]

1. *Tegestologist*—A collector of beer mats.
2. *Terpsichorean*—Related to dance.
3. *Thewless*—Cowardly, lacking energy.
4. *Tintinnabulation*—The ringing of bells.
5. *Toddle*—To walk in a carefree way, walk like a little child.
6. *Toxophilite*—A lover of archery.
7. *Transuranic*—The highly unstable elements at the bottom of the Periodic Table.
8. *Triskaidekaphobia*—Fear of the number thirteen.
9. *Tushery*—The use of archaic language in one's writing.
10. *Tyromancy*—Foretelling the future by examining cheese.

---

[76] No special reason. I would note though that I wanted to include *borborygmous* here but unfortunately it doesn't begin with T.

Thesaurus

What's another word for thesaurus?
—Unknown

Given my early interest in words I am embarrassed to confess that I first learned about a thesaurus only in Standard 9, the equivalent/equal/counterpart/parallel of one's junior year in high school. Somehow, I thought I should have encountered one much sooner. This treasury of synonyms (with some antonyms thrown in for extra helpfulness) is a boon for any writer.

The concept of collecting synonyms wasn't new; that honor goes to one of the ancient Greeks, Phylo of Byblos. Other compilations were made, in various languages. The concept finally gained traction in English thanks to Peter Roget, an English physician and scholar. He is now regarded as the founding father of the modern English-language thesaurus. Curiously (oddly/strangely/unusually), he wrote it in 1805 but didn't publish it until 1852.

The word thesaurus is derived from Latin, which in turn had stolen it from Greek. The original Greek meant "treasure, treasury or storehouse." And that's certainly what a thesaurus provides (gives/imparts/supplies).

Tongue Twisters

We tend to outgrow our fascination with tongue-twisters fairly early, certainly by our teens. But they're fun while they last. Here is reputedly the most difficult in English, according to the *Guinness Book of World Records*. (As with all tongue-twisters, say it as fast as possible, and repeat as fast as possible.)

- *The sixth sick sheik's sixth sheep's sick.*

Not so, say researchers at the Massachusetts Institute of Technology. They say this sentence (which sounds meaninglessness to me) is even more difficult:

- *Pad kid poured curd pulled cod.*

Here are five more with which you can torment members of your family or assess candidates in a job interview:

- *Is this a zither? This is a zither.*
- *The new nuns knew the true nuns knew the new nuns too.*
- *The rat ran by the river with a lump of raw liver.*
- *The seething sea ceaseth and thus the seething sea sufficeth us.*
- *Shep Schwab shopped at Scott's Schnapps shop;*
- *One shot of Scott's Schnapps stopped Schwab's watch.*

Tricky Words

Go on, admit it: certain words or word pairs always leave you flummoxed. Or at least, you have to think hard about keeping their meanings apart. The **Errors List** identified some of my students' weak spots. Now, in a gesture of unexpected self-disclosure, I am including my own list of head-scratchers. No matter how often I check these words, I still have at least a touch of insecurity, hesitation, or continuing downright confusion on their meanings. [Thinks: Maybe putting these in writing for the world to see will help me get a better handle on them.]

***

As if/Like: Let's deal first with *like*, which is a preposition and introduces a simple object. "She dances *like* Margot Fonteyn." *Like* cannot introduce a clause. By contrast, *as if* functions as a conjunction and can introduce a clause: "It looks *as if* we'll have to cancel the group photo." Over the years we've been bombarded with confusion between the two, as in the cigarette ad, "Winston tastes good *like* a cigarette should." But you can't have that verb "should" following the *like*.

***

Convince/Persuade: To persuade someone is to talk him or her into doing or believing something. "I *persuaded* you to come hang-gliding with us." By contrast, to be *convinced* is a state of certainty or confidence about a matter. "I am *convinced* I can win the election." If I try to *persuade* you, and succeed, you will end up being *convinced*.

***

Discreet/Discrete: I know the difference between them, but I am never sure which is which. OK, here goes: *Discreet* means keeping things confidential, or showing good judgment. "The lawyer was suitably *discreet* in handling my blackmail problem." It also means not being noticed, as in "My private eye followed the blackmailer at a *discreet* distance." Then, *discrete* means distinct or separate. "The words *convince* and *persuade* have *discrete* meanings."

***

Loath/Loathe: As with the previous entry, here too I know the two different meanings but don't know which is which. To start with, *loath* is an adjective, meaning reluctant to, while *loathe* is a verb that means detest or hate. "I am *loath* to travel with that abominable woman." "I *loathe* my half-brother after he cheated me out of my inheritance."

***

None: "Tell me, Master: Does this word take a singular or plural verb? How can I know for sure?"

And the Master said that it all depends on the meaning of *none*.

"Tell me more," I replied.

"When *none* means 'no one' or 'not one,' then use a singular verb. If *none* means 'no two, no amount or no number,' go with the plural."

I responded, "It's that simple?"

He nodded.

"Can you give me some examples," I asked.

"Because you are an eager learner, my child, I will honor your request," the Master said. "*None* of the passengers was injured." He explained that none in this sentence clearly meant not one. "*None* of the taxes were paid." Here the sense is "no amount."

***

Rebut/Refute: Rebut is to take a stand against something someone has said or written. "The mayor *rebutted* the council member's charge that he had used city funds without authorization." Note: It doesn't mean the mayor was successful; it just means she tried. If you succeed in destroying the claim, then you have *refuted* it.

***

There are others. But I think I have bared enough of my soul for now.

Typos

One letter can make the world of difference, as an educational institution learned to its acute embarrassment in 2012. The Lyndon B. Johnson School of Public Affairs, at the University of Texas in Austin, published its commencement brochure describing itself as "The School of Pubic Affairs." The School duly issued an apology for what it termed its "eggregious typo." Hey, leave out one letter here, add another one there; it'll all come out OK in the end.

Jane Milizia, a copy editor for *The Burlington Free Press*, noted an error in a recipe for "refrigerator cookies." It should have read "Wrap in foil and store in the refrigerator." However, a C had replaced the W in "wrap." Fortunately, she caught the error before press time.

Another northeast newspaper, *The New Haven Connecticut Register*, wasn't as lucky. Its blunder, which made it into print, concerned a story about the amount of legislation the governor had signed into law. Nobody noticed until after they had gone to press that there was no space between "pen" and "is" in the headline: "Governor's Pen Is Busy."

One of the most celebrated typos of all time came in a biblical misprint that had major ramifications, potentially for the morals of society and most certainly for the printers responsible. In what became known as *The Wicked Bible*, a printing of the *King James Version* of the Bible in 1631 included a typo for the commandment, "Thou shalt not commit adultery." (Exodus 20:14) The "not" was omitted. The authorities were not amused and fined the printers £300, a crippling sum, and took away their printing license. Most copies were destroyed and the few that remain are now highly valued collectors' items.

That wasn't the only major biblical misprint, however. A 1716 Bible had Jeremiah 31:34, "Sin no more," appear as "Sin on more."

One of my favorite typos was local. A Spokane music organization was promoting a music festival, boasting of a twelve-hour continuous *recital*. But their printed material instead dropped the I in recital—thus offering a radically different experience.

***

Copy editors learn early on to watch for words like "public," as the University of Texas experience shows. But even seemingly innocent words, like *not* can be problematic if they're one letter off. "Gordon Jackson is *not* a drug pusher" could easily become "Gordon Jackson is *now* a drug pusher."

Unspoken Words

In **Words that Stir** you'll find some examples of powerful oratory delivered by leaders in times of crisis. But what of powerful speeches that were *not* delivered? William Safire was a speech writer for Richard Nixon at the time of the first moon landing in 1969. He wanted the president to be prepared for an awful prospect: What if the Apollo 11 crew of Neil Armstrong and Buzz Aldrin could not return to the command module piloted by Michael Collins?

Safire wrote the following speech for Nixon to use in case the moon landing ended in disaster. Fortunately, the speech wasn't needed but it's a piece of writing that is well worth reading.

***

Fate has ordained that the men who went to the moon to explore in peace will stay on the moon to rest in peace.

These brave men, Neil Armstrong and Edwin Aldrin, know that there is no hope for their recovery. But they also know that there is hope for mankind in their sacrifice.

These two men are laying down their lives in mankind's most noble goal: the search for truth and understanding.

They will be mourned by their families and friends; they will be mourned by their nation; they will be mourned by the people of the world; they will be mourned by a Mother Earth that dared send two of her sons into the unknown.

In their exploration, they stirred the people of the world to feel as one; in their sacrifice, they bind more tightly the brotherhood of man.

In ancient days, men looked at stars and saw their heroes in the constellations. In modern times, we do much the same, but our heroes are epic men of flesh and blood.

Others will follow, and surely find their way home. Man's search will not be denied. But these men were the first, and they will remain the foremost in our hearts.

For every human being who looks up at the moon in the nights to come will know that there is some corner of another world that is forever mankind.

Weak Words—And Their Antidote

I once had a student who unwittingly used the word *very* fourteen times in a single typed page. All I needed to do was highlight the word in yellow, driving home the point that this weak word detracted from her writing, having just the opposite effect she hoped for. That's the problem with weak words. On the one hand, they add little or nothing to our writing or speech. On the other, they undermine it. Using *very* once or twice in a 1,500-word term paper will not be noticed. Using it fourteen times in one page will.

What else should you cut from your repertoire? *Really* is another piece of deadwood. So is *actually*. Take "I was *really* surprised that he *actually* ate six Big Macs in a row." Both can go.

Watch too for weak adjectives, like *nice*. Let's say I ask someone how his summer was and he says, "Oh, I had a nice time in Des Moines." I could leave it at that, accepting a wishy-washy word that tells me only that he viewed the experience positively. If I push him and asked, "Why do you say that?" he might go one level deeper: "Well, I got to see some family members I hadn't seen in a while, and we got to go snipe hunting."[77] You've prodded him to say a lot more and you in turn have learned more as well.

---

[77] A snipe hunt, according to Wikipedia, is a type of practical joke or fool's errand, in existence in North America as early as the 1840s, in which an unsuspecting newcomer is duped into trying to catch a nonexistent animal called a snipe.

The questions "Why do you say that?" and "Can you please tell me more about that?" are powerful tools for eliciting deeper levels of information from someone using weak wording.

Example:

> *"Congressman, what do you think of the President's proposal to ban Halloween?"*
>
> *"Well, Bob, I think it's a bad idea."*
>
> *"Why do you say that?"*
>
> *"Well, Bob, many kids will be disappointed—bitterly disappointed."*
>
> *"Please tell me more about that."*
>
> *"Well, Bob, my own children are devastated at the possibility they won't be able to go trick or treating this year."*
>
> *"Why do you say that?"*
>
> *"Well, Bob, my little Abigail, who's 4, was so looking forward to going dressed as a vacuum cleaner. She's already got this great costume. And Buddy, who's 6, is planning to go dressed as a rabid porcupine. Well, Bob, gotta run. Thank you."*
>
> *"Actually, it's Jennifer. But you're welcome."*

Note how much more Jennifer got in the interview for pushing the Congressman beyond "a bad idea." The moral of the story: if someone's using weak words, push, push, push for more (politely, of course).[78]

***

True confession: I have my own list of weak words. One of them is *simply*, as in "We had invited his holiness the Pope to Brian's birthday party but he simply didn't show up." As I am working on this manuscript, I have already searched for *simply* and found three instances where it's simply not needed. *Um... not*

---

[78] It seems fitting in this section to have a meaningless footnote, like this one.

needed. Another is *pretty,* as in *"pretty* good." (I just found a few, one of which I removed and another I thought would be OK.)

When I finish a complete draft I'll check *simply* and *pretty* again, and do likewise for *very, really* and *actually.* That's for two reasons. One is to strengthen the writing. The other is to avoid being caught out as a hypocrite and not practicing what I preach.[79] Everyone loves exposing a hypocrite and, insofar as I can, I want to deprive you of that pleasure.

See also **Meaningless Words**.

---

[79] Isn't "practicing what you preach" a cliché? You betcha. Given what I wrote in **Clichés**, didn't you enjoy the deliberate irony?

When Words Fail

Communication is the art of being understood.
　—Peter Ustinov

It's not enough for *you* to know what you mean when you're using words to communicate; whoever is on the receiving end needs to grasp your meaning. Think back to the Introduction and the confusion I had over the word *shed*. My friend knew what he meant when he used a word unfamiliar to me, but I didn't. If you're not understood, you haven't successfully communicated. Here are two more examples.

The first is of someone who is so engrossed in her style of conveying information that she fails to grasp the point of the TV interview: to convey clear, factual information in a way that would be understood by the viewers. Clark Whelton, a former speech writer for New York Mayors Ed Koch and Rudy Guliani, wrote an essay in 2011 titled "What Happens in Vagueness Stays in Vagueness—The decline and fall of American English, and stuff." Here's the opening paragraph.

I recently watched a television program in which a woman described a baby squirrel that she had found in her yard. "And he was like, you know, 'Helloooo, what are you looking at?' and stuff, and I'm like, you know, 'Can I, like, pick you up?,' and he goes, like, 'Brrrp brrrp,' and I'm like, you know, 'Whoa, that is so wow!' " She rambled on, speaking in self-quotations, sound effects, and other vocabulary substitutes, punctuating her sentences with facial tics and lateral eye shifts. All the while, however, she never said anything specific about her encounter with the squirrel.

***

Whelton went on to lament the lack of clarity and specificity in the writing of college graduates he encountered. Interviewing interns, this is what he encountered:

> *I asked a candidate where she went to school.*
> *"Columbia?" she replied. Or asked.*
> *"And you're majoring in . . ."*
> *"English?"*
> *All her answers sounded like questions. Several other students did the same thing, ending declarative sentences with an interrogative rise.*

***

Then he noted how many of the young people he spoke to would narrate both sides of a conversation: "So I'm like, 'Want to, like, see a movie?' And he goes, 'No way.' And I go . . ."

Such incoherence is hardly effective in getting one's message across with clarity and ensuring that your hearer will get your point.

***

The second example involves a friend who during his graduate studies was walking on campus, on a path often used by cyclists as well. He heard a voice behind him yelling "Left." Assuming it was someone on a bike coming up behind him, he stepped to his left—and straight into her path, causing her to crash into him. What was obvious to her ("I intend to pass you on your left") wasn't obvious to my friend. She knew what she meant but incorrectly assumed he would know too.

Like Squirrel Lady, the cyclist knew what she wanted to convey. But for quite different reasons, her use of words proved equally ineffective, and potentially dangerous. The lesson? The first law of communications bears repeating: How your words are perceived is as important (even more so, perhaps) as what you intended to convey. As Montaigne put it, "The word is half his that speaks, and half his that hears it." If that second half is missing, your words have failed you.

Who/Whom

Calvin Trillin, a writer for *The New Yorker* magazine, said: "As far as I'm concerned, *'whom'* is a word that was invented to make everyone sound like a butler." To a degree, journalism professor George Arnold agrees with Trillin's assessment that ordinary English speakers don't bother with the word. Writing in the *Media Writer's Handbook*, he concedes that "Most people who speak and write in English have no problem deciding when to use *whom* instead of *who*. They gave *whom* the old heave-ho a long time ago. And they gave *whomever* the same treatment."

Yet Arnold says that *who* and *whom* exist, "and like it or not, professional writers must be knowledgeable about when to use them." The same goes for those of us who prize careful and accurate grammar in our speech. Let's take this in three steps.

To begin with, we need to know the different functions of the words. *Who* and *whoever* are subjects, *whom* and *whomever* are objects. We need to use *whom* and *whomever* when they are the object of a verb or preposition. We know this intuitively, at least to some degree. We are unlikely to write or say, "<u>Whom</u> is your favorite movie star?" or "To <u>who</u> should I speak about the goldfish?"

However, things are not always as simple in practice, possibly on those rare occasions when you encounter a sentence with a reticulating subverbal interrogative.[80] No, the real problem is when we add an extra clause or two to a sentence. For example:

The company president gave bonuses to all sales staff <u>*who/whom*</u> *their managers recommended.* Now what?

---

[80] I just made that up.

Let's do this in four steps.[81]

1. Isolate the clause that contains the *who/whom* option. So we have *who/whom their managers recommended.*

2. Rearrange the wording to make a simple statement: *Their managers recommended ......*

3. Now ask, would we complete this with either a subjective or objective pronoun (remember the difference?). So we'd have either *Their managers recommended they* OR *Their managers recommended them.*

4. You make your choice, which is now obvious. It's become clear that you need *them*, the objective form. (You wouldn't say *Their managers recommended they.*)

That means your original sentence needs *whom*, the objective form: *The company president gave bonuses to all sales staff whom their managers recommended.*

Here's another approach. Remember that *who* parallels *he* and *they*—and they all end in a vowel or a vowel sound (*they*). Then, *whom* parallels *him* and *them*; they all end in M. So if you are thinking of writing, "*Who* is your favorite actor?" you can resolve the *who/whom* issue by saying, "*He* is your favorite actor." Both *who* and *he* end in a vowel. (You wouldn't say "*Him* is your favorite actor" or "*Them* are your favorite comedians.")

Likewise with *whom*: "To *whom* should I speak about the goldfish?" You could answer that by saying, "I will speak to *him* about the goldfish." You need the parallel endings in M.

---

[81] This four-step approach is taken from *The Penguin Handbook* (2nd edition), by Lester Faigley. In case a clarification is needed, this book has nothing to do with penguins or their care. If you are seeking a book about actual penguins, I'd highly recommend Tom Michell's charming account of his encounter with the Magellan penguin that he rescued in Argentina, titled *The Penguin Lessons.*

***

If these ideas don't help in your situation, your last option is to avoid the *who/whom* problem altogether, if you can, by rewording a sentence. Take our earlier example:

The company president gave bonuses to all sales staff <u>*who/whom*</u> *their managers recommended.*

How about: *The company president gave bonuses to all sales staff if their managers had recommended them.*

Only I will know of your subterfuge and I won't tell.

The Wonderful O

The Wonderful O is a wonderful book. It is the product of the ingenious mind of James Thurber, a cartoonist, playwright and author who gained fame initially as a writer for *The New Yorker* magazine. *The Wonderful O* was the last in his series of children's fairy tales. The villain in the story, a pirate, demands that the letter O not be used among the island community where he believes the treasure is hidden. This lack of the letter becomes a vehicle for Thurber's exquisite word play as the story unfolds, in which only words without an O are permitted on the island. I remember as a teenager being entranced at the high wire writing act that this author was engaged in. Here are two brief excerpts. A poet in the community speaks to the townspeople at a secret meeting as they lament the ban on words with the letter O.

> *"Soon Black and Littlejack," said Andreus, "will no longer let us live in houses, for houses have an O."*
>
> *"Or cottages," said the blacksmith, "for cottage has an O, and so does bungalow."*
>
> *"We'll have to live in huts," the baker said, "or shacks, or sheds, or shanties, or in cabins."*
>
> *"Cabins without logs," said Andreus. "We shall have mantels but no clocks, shelves without crocks, keys without locks, walls without doors, rugs without floors, frames without windows, chimneys without roofs to put them on, knives without a fork or spoon, beds without pillows. There will be no wood for our fires, no oil for our lamps, and no hobs for our kettles."*

***

The theater in the town was closed, for Shakespeare's lines without an O sound were flat and muffled. No one could play Othello *when* Othello *turned to* Thell, *and Desdemona was strangled at the start.... Spoken words became a hissing and a mumble, or a murmur and a hum. A man named Otto Ott, when asked his name, could only stutter.*

***

Thurber chose to write the book in the form of a lipogram, an example of what is known as "constrained writing." In this case, it entailed Thurber choosing to omit certain letters from all the words affecting the island community. And as the excerpts indicate, Thurber also had fun with alliteration and rhyme. He uses these techniques throughout the book, which is all the more impressive given the constraints he imposed on himself.

***

Many forms of poetry also require a strict format to be followed. Think of a sonnet, for example, the most common form of which runs to fourteen lines and has to follow a strict rhyme structure, or a haiku, made of three lines with five, seven and five syllables in each.

Regarding constrained writing, former US poet laureate Billy Collins spoofed a difficult French form of poetry known as a villanelle by inventing what he called the paradelle, another form of verse, from eleventh century France. Initially, people believed the paradelle was a genuine, and impossibly difficult, form to follow. But then more people realized it was a joke, partly because Collins' own example of a paradelle was awful. The first stanza ended with this nonsensical line: "Darken the mountain, time and find was my into it was with to to"—which should have tipped off readers that as gifted a poet like Collins had to be kidding.

That's a far cry from my favorite Collins poem, "Another Reason Why I Don't Keep a Gun in the House," about his neighbors' dog that won't stop barking. While playing a Beethoven symphony at full blast to drown out the barking, Colins imagines Beethoven incorporating the dog into one of his masterpieces. The concluding lines refer to "the famous barking dog solo that... first established Beethoven as an innovative genius."[82]

---

[82] Yes, yes—I admit we're drifting here; this is hardly related to Thurber's book. But if you go and read this poem I'm confident you'll agree this digression was worthwhile.

Word Games

My wife and I worked at the same university for an extended period and sometimes ended up in the same committee meetings. To enliven them, at least for ourselves, we would lay down a challenge before the meeting: Try to weave into the discussion, unobtrusively and naturally, some obscure word. No prizes were awarded if we succeeded and there was no judge whose decision was final. But it was an interesting way to pass those committee hours.

Another game we have enjoyed, known to us as "Dictionary," requires a small group and a good dictionary. Someone looks up an obscure word, checks that nobody in the group knows it, and then invites everyone to make up the most convincing definition. These definitions, along with the real one, are read to the group and huge prizes are given to those who guess the correct definition.[83] The game has now been made available commercially as Balderdash, which saves you looking up the words.

Like us, people have been playing words games of all kinds, presumably as long as people have had words. Some are board games; others need only pencil and paper, like Hangman. For brevity's sake let list just four commercially available games.

Balderdash—See the description above.
Bananagrams—A fast-paced game using Scrabble-like tiles to make words. Unlike **Scrabble**, one can undo and rearrange words.

---

[83] Not really. On an unrelated note, I want to point out that I haven't mentioned *borborygmous* in a while.

<u>Bethumped with Words</u>—A Trivial Pursuit-style game but all about words. It takes its name from a quote from Shakespeare, "Zounds! I was never so bethump'd with words...." One of our family's favorites.

<u>Boggle</u>—You have to identify words that are embedded in a set of sixteen dice, each with letters on them. Racing against the clock, you see which adjoining letters can be formed into words.[84]

***

If you want to explore another medium, and do some good at the same time, take a look at the Free Rice website: freerice.com. Affiliated with the United Nations' World Food Program, it relies on sponsors to contribute a few grains of rice for every vocabulary word you can identify correctly. The game has graduated levels of difficulty, starting with the simplest of words and progressing to fiendishly difficult ones.

---

[84] Why do all these games begin with the letter B? No idea.

Words about Words

- *Anaphora*—A rhetorical device that consists of repeating words at the beginning of subsequent lines. An excellent example is the beginning of Charles Dickens' *A Tale of Two Cities*: "It was the best of times, it was the worst of times, it was the age of wisdom, it was the age of foolishness, it was the epoch of belief, it was the epoch of incredulity, it was the season of Light, it was the season of Darkness, it was the spring of hope, it was the winter of despair."

- *Antimetabole*—A repetition of words or an idea in a reverse order. For example, "To fail to plan is to plan to fail."

- *Contronym*—A word with contradictory meanings, like *cleave* (cut in half or stick together) or *sanction* (permit or prohibit).

- *Crackjaw*—A word or phrase that's hard to pronounce.

- *Etymology*—The origin of words. OK, you most likely knew this one, but it's included as a pretext to include this Tweet from writer and voice actor Gemma Amor: "The fact that some people can't distinguish between *etymology* and *entomology* bugs me in ways I can't put into words."

- *Holophrasm*—A one-word sentence, for example, *Go.* Or a complex idea conveyed in a single word, such as *Howdy* for "How do you do?"

- *Logodaedaly*—Skill in using or coining words.

- *Logophile*—A lover of words.

- *Logophilia*—The love of words.

- *Metonomy*—A figure of speech consisting of the use of a name of one thing for that of another, with which it is associated, such as "Capitol Hill" for the US Congress or the "Crown" for the Queen.
- *Monologophobia*—The fear of using the same word within three lines, lest you seem limited in your vocabulary. This is the sort of obsession that could lead to something like, "God said, 'Let there be light,' and there was solar illumination.'"
- *Mot juste*—The right word.
- *Onomatomania*—An obsession with particular words or names and the desire to recall or repeat them.
- *Polysemous*—An adjective describing a word that has more than one meaning.
- *Progressive Words*—Words formed from left to right, such as *to/tot/tote/totem.* (See *Regressive Words*)
- *Regressive Words*—Words formed from right to left, such as *ate/late/elate/relate.* (See *Progressive Words*)
- *Rhopalism*—A snowball sentence. It starts with a one-letter word and adds a letter with each successive word. For example, "I do not know where family doctors acquired illegibly perplexing handwriting; nevertheless, extraordinary pharmaceutical intellectuality counter-balancing indecipherability transcendentalizes intercommunications' incomprehensibleness." (With *incomprehensibleness* increasingly becoming the operative word....)
- *Syllepsis*—A construction in which a word governs two or more other words but agrees in number, gender or case with only one of them, or has a different meaning when applied to each word. Phew... An example, *please*: "He lost his coat and his temper."
- *Tmesis*— Stuffing a word into the middle of another, such as *a-whole-nother, to-us- wards* or *unlikely* changed into *un-bloody-likely.*

- *Tosspot Word*—A new word formed by placing a noun after a verb, in which the verb acts on the noun. For example, *pickpocket* and *breakfast.*
- *Zeugma*—A figure of speech in which a word applies to two others in different senses, for example, "John and his license expired last week" or to two others of which it semantically suits only one, for example, "With weeping eyes and hearts."

See also **Eggcorns**, **Eponyms**, **Mondegreens**, **Onomatopoeia**, **Oxymorons**, **Palindromes** and **Pangrams**.

Words that Stir

Adlai Stevenson was a prominent Democrat who served as governor of Illinois and twice ran unsuccessfully for president against Dwight Eisenhower in the 1950s. Once when he was complimented on a speech he'd delivered, he said people commented that he made nice speeches. But, he observed, when John F. Kennedy made a speech, they said, "Let's march!"

Certain orators have the gift for moving people, through their own words or more recently through those of their speech writers. Here are half a dozen of especially powerful statements from leaders.

***

Susan B. Anthony

It was we, the people; not we, the white male citizens; nor yet we, the male citizens; but we, the whole people, who formed the Union. And we formed it, not to give the blessings of liberty, but to secure them; not to the half of ourselves and the half of our posterity, but to the whole people—women as well as men. And it is a downright mockery to talk to women of their enjoyment of the blessings of liberty while they are denied the use of the only means of securing them provided by this democratic-republican government—the ballot.

For any state to make sex a qualification that must ever result in the disfranchisement of one entire half of the people, is to pass a bill of attainder, or, an ex post facto law, and is therefore a violation of the supreme law of the land. By it the blessings of liberty are forever withheld from women and their female posterity....

The only question left to be settled now is: Are women persons? And I hardly believe any of our opponents will have the hardihood to say they are not. Being persons, then, women are citizens; and no state has a right to make any law, or to enforce any old law, that shall abridge their privileges or immunities. Hence, every discrimination against women in the constitutions and laws of the several states is today null and void, precisely as is every one against Negroes.

—In a speech for casting a vote in the 1872 presidential election, for which she was fined $100, and which she refused to pay

***

Winston Churchill

We have before us an ordeal of the most grievous kind. We have before us many, many long months of struggle and of suffering. You ask, what is our policy? I can say: It is to wage war, by sea, land and air, with all our might and with all the strength that God can give us; to wage war against a monstrous tyranny, never surpassed in the dark, lamentable catalogue of human crime. That is our policy. You ask, what is our aim? I can answer in one word: It is victory, victory at all costs, victory in spite of all terror, victory, however long and hard the road may be; for without victory, there is no survival. Let that be realized; no survival for the British Empire, no survival for all that the British Empire has stood for, no survival for the urge and impulse of the ages, that mankind will move forward towards its goal. But I take up my task with buoyancy and hope. I feel sure that our cause will not be suffered to fail among men. At this time I feel entitled to claim the aid of all, and I say, "Come then, let us go forward together with our united strength."

—Speech to the House of Commons, May 13, 1940, as he sought to form a unity government to take on the Nazi war effort

222

***

Winston Churchill

Even though large tracts of Europe and many old and famous States have fallen or may fall into the grip of the Gestapo and all the odious apparatus of Nazi rule, we shall not flag or fail. We shall go on to the end, we shall fight in France, we shall fight on the seas and oceans, we shall fight with growing confidence and growing strength in the air, we shall defend our Island, whatever the cost may be, we shall fight on the beaches, we shall fight on the landing grounds, we shall fight in the fields and in the streets, we shall fight in the hills; we shall never surrender, and even if, which I do not for a moment believe, this Island or a large part of it were subjugated and starving, then our Empire beyond the seas, armed and guarded by the British Fleet, would carry on the struggle, until, in God's good time, the New World, with all its power and might, steps forth to the rescue and the liberation of the old.

— Speech to the House of Commons, May 13, 1940, following the mostly successful evacuation of British troops from Dunkirk in France

***

John Fitzgerald Kennedy

Ask not what your country can do for you—ask what you can do for your country.

—Inaugural address, Jan. 20. 1961

***

John Fitzgerald Kennedy

We choose to go to the moon and do these other things, not because they are easy, but because they are hard.

—Sept. 12, 1962

***

Abraham Lincoln

With malice toward none; with charity for all; with firmness in the right, as God gives us to see the right, let us strive on to finish the work we are in; to bind up the nation's wounds; to care for him who shall have borne the battle, and for his widow, and his orphan—to do all which may achieve and cherish a just, and a lasting peace, among ourselves, and with all nations.

—Second inaugural address, March 4, 1865

***

Franklin D. Roosevelt

The only thing we have to fear is fear itself.

— Inaugural address, March 4, 1933

See also **Unspoken Words** for a speech that was not given.

And the Word Was With God

In the beginning was the Word, and the Word was with God, and the Word was God.
    —*The Gospel of John 1:1*

Central to the Christian faith is the belief that Jesus was both fully divine and fully human, and was in fact God incarnate. No other major religion hinges on the dual claim that God became human and, in the form of Jesus, sacrificed himself to save people from their sins. But why does John begin his gospel by describing Jesus as "the Word"?

The Greek word is *logos*, which had great significance for the two audiences John's gospel would reach: Greeks and Jews. *The New International Version Study Bible* says of this word that "Greeks used this term not only of the spoken word but also of the unspoken word, the word still in the mind—the reason. When they applied it to the universe, they meant the rational principle that governs all things. Jews, on the other hand, used it as a way of referring to God. Thus John used a term that was meaningful to both Jews and Gentiles."[85]

We can say at least two other things about John's choice of words. First, a *word* is about communication; it has an inherent meaning for us to interpret and understand. In this case, Christians believe, Jesus was the Word—God himself—revealed to humankind. Just as words make tangible our unspoken thoughts, so did Jesus make the invisible God visible through his incarnation.

---

[85] Notes on John 1:1 in *The New International Version Study Bible*.

Second, in addition to who he was, he had a Word to share: to tell us through his life and teaching what God is like and what he expects of us.

At the risk of seeming flippant, it is as if God intervened in history and tapped humanity on the shoulder and said, "Listen up, I have a Word for you."

Yes, We Have a Word for That

This section could go on almost indefinitely. Entire books of unusual words are available if you need more. The dozen entries below are included to reinforce the point that has been made repeatedly in this book: that English is a splendidly diverse language. Its array of words covers a vocabulary so overwhelmingly large that no one person could master it. Fortunately, we don't have to. Most of us get by with just a few thousand words and find they are enough to lead rich and fulfilling lives.

Our lives, though, can be just that much richer as we discover just the perfect word for what we need to say—a word we didn't even know existed.

1. *Accubation*—Eating or drinking while lying down.
2. *Callipygian*—Having a shapely butt.
3. *Dactylion*—The tip of the middle finger.
4. *Darg*—A day's work.
5. *Griffonage*—Careless or illegible handwriting.
6. *Krukolibidinous*—The act of looking at someone's crotch.
7. *Livelock*—A jargon term in computing for a state in which two processes each continually change their state in response to changes in the other without either doing anything useful.
8. *Pandiculation*—Yawning and stretching at the same time.

9. *Paresthesia*—The prickly feeling when your limb "falls asleep."[86]
10. *Pilgarlic*—Having a bald head; also a pitiable or foolish person.[87]
11. *Ruderous*—Filled with garbage.
12. *Symphoric*—Accident-prone.

---

[86] The comedian, Steven Wright, said: "I hate it when my foot falls asleep during the day because that means it's going to be up all night."

[87] I take offense at Wiktionary's putting those two definitions side by side, as I fit only one of them.

Conclusion—An Appetite for Battle

Know in advance that the fight for careful language is probably a losing one, but at the same time don't allow this knowledge to take the edge off your appetite for battle.
—Joseph Epstein

That's how Epstein, a literature professor at Northwestern University,[88] concluded an essay titled "The Joys and Sorrows of Being a Word Snob." He insisted on the need to use words carefully. I agree. There's a reason, as noted in **The *Right* Word**, that we have *torturous* (relating to torture) and *tortuous* (twisting, complex). Same with *uninterested* (indifferent, just not interested) and *disinterested* (impartial, neutral).

Some words are worth fighting for, and others worth fighting against. *Unique* is featured in the **Errors List** because many of my students incorrectly assumed it can be modified to *very unique* or *somewhat unique*. I plan to keep defending its meaning.

Likewise with *niggardly*. Even though this is a touchy word, given that it *sounds* something like the ultra-taboo N-word, its meaning and etymology have nothing to do with racism. I'd be extremely careful of the settings in which I'd use it, given the hyper-sensitivity audiences or readers have about it. But I still want to assert my right to use this word when it's appropriate (even if it's only as an example in a book about words).

***

Where have I given up? I long ago stopped insisting that *fun* is a noun and not acceptable as an adjective. So even though I

---

[88] In Evanston, Illinois, near Chicago. Not to be confused with other institutions with similar names.

still try to avoid saying something like, "We had a *fun* time at the abattoir," I concede that this battle is lost and *fun*-the-adjective has now weaseled its way into standard English.

It's the same with *impact* as a verb. Many writers turn up their noses at "The drought will negatively *impact* tax revenues." This is now widely enough accepted that I just shrug and let it go.

Next is *good* and *well*. If you ask me how I am, and I say, "I'm *good*," I am in good company but I am grammatically in error. Strictly speaking, I have just told you about my moral condition rather than my health. I should have said (assuming I am in robust physical and mental health) "I am *well*, thank you." *The Associated Press Stylebook* says that "*Good* is an adjective that means something is as it should be or is better than average. When used as an adjective, *well* means suitable, proper, healthy. When used as an adverb, *well* means in a satisfactory manner or skillfully." You can say "I feel good" if you mean, "I'm in good health." And if you say, "I feel well," it suggests your sense of touch is working good. Um... well.

But trying to keep the lines clear between *good* and *well* was lost long ago. Same with *decimate*, which was a useful word meaning "to kill every tenth person." Now for many people it just means "destroy" or "inflict heavy damage."

***

I am still trying to fight the good fight on another front, though. Even though I side with those good writers who persist in honoring subject-pronoun agreement, I concede this is a losing battle, as we are hemorrhaging troops left and right on this one. Let's take "A student should prepare for his or her exam." Clunky, yes, but the noun and pronoun agree. I'd prefer "Students should prepare for their exam" (same noun-pronoun agreement, so all is well). But what is increasingly acceptable, even in what we might call "good" writing, is "A student should prepare for their exams." *Student/their*? Hold your horses, buster... Isn't there a rule against that?

I had a colleague who was an editor with old school standards. She was so insistent on correct usage that she upended decades of practice in the college from which she graduated. Her diploma, like thousands distributed previously, had a grammatical error that she insisted be corrected. And it was, for her—and all future graduates. When she approached retirement from her editing job, I chatted with her about this noun-pronoun agreement issue. She said with resignation that she expected that on her last day at work, as she drove out of the parking lot, her junior colleagues would immediately ditch this rule and breathe a sigh of relief. She was probably right.

***

Then there's the fight-against category. Let's begin with *irregardless*. Even though Merriam-Webster accords it grudging recognition,[89] based on the fact that it actually gets used, it's an abomination that needs to be barred entry at the city gates.

Another is *literally*, which means just that: something that is factually true. Don't say, "My divorce lawyer was literally a tiger in the courtroom." No, he wasn't.

Lastly, let's rally support for *notorious*, which a troubling number of people equate with famous or well-known. Someone with a *notorious* reputation is well known but for negative reasons. It grates to read, "Anthea Athletic was *notorious* for the number of high school and college track records she set." Not so; she was *famous* or *well known* or *renowned*. Charles Manson was *notorious*.

***

I accept that English is a dynamic language, with rules and usage perpetually in flux. That's fine. But while the democratic masses (of whom I am one) are slowly reshaping various parts of the language, as they are entitled to do, I remain adamant that we need *some* rules and need to set *some* standards. Yes, they may change over time. But they are the rules and

---

[89] See also Kori Stamper's marvelous book, *Word by Word*, which has a chapter dedicated to this word. See **Dictionaries**.

standards which, for good or ill, we happen to have right now. For me, a good rule of thumb is, "Would I correct my children's speech or writing on this point?" Or what would I tell my students is acceptable use in the marketplace they aspire to enter? Even a mediocre boss wouldn't tolerate *irregardless*.[90]

Fortunately, I have attained a perfect balance between a stuffy insistence on outdated rules, on the one hand, and a cavalier tolerance, on the other, that in reality stands for nothing. Or, to put it in the form of a **Russell Conjugation**: *I defend sensible language usage. You are a pedant. He is a word Nazi.*

I expanded on my thoughts about word usage in my novel, *Never Say "Moist" at Wyndover College.* These thoughts come from a retired professor commenting on what words should be acceptable on campus, and which should be banned. Professor Bauerbach served as a useful vehicle for outlining the essence of my view of words. This is what I had him say:

> *"Words," he wrote, "are sacred and powerful things. We are human because of words. Yes, other species have ways of communicating with each other, but we humans do so with an astonishing complexity."*
>
> *He offered some examples: "Our language equips us to cover the most diverse set of interactions. Two surgeons are discussing in the operating theatre which procedure to pursue in a complicated case. A dying grandfather telling his extended family one by one how much he loves them, and how they must grieve sensibly, not too long or too hard, once he has died. Or two Wyndover students, an engaged couple holding hands as they sit in Jenkins Wood on the fringe of campus, dreaming about a lifetime together."*
>
> *"Words," he said, "are precious things, even the unlovely ones, those that hurt or trouble us. Even they have their place. See them if you will as the mosquitoes or rattlesnakes of our vocabulary; we don't seek them out, but we must*

---

[90] I hope....

acknowledge that they have their place in the ecology of our language. We should not seek to extinguish them. Nor should we tell others which words they may or may not include in their vocabulary."

"Of course, we should be prudent and sensitive to others. As a matter of grace, we must be careful not to hurt them, either by deliberate provocation with our word choice or by thoughtless insensitivity in not taking their feelings into account. But these should be our choices, not those of others telling us what belongs in our vocabulary and what doesn't."[91]

***

Linguist David Crystal makes an important point about the need for applying grammar, usage and other rules with flexibility. Referring to writing, he says, "Competent writers know they have the ability to switch into and out of standard English," what we might define as "good" English—that which we'd expect to see in a well-edited book, newspaper or magazine. He adds, "This is one of the linguistic skills that children have to be taught." We use different kinds of speech and writing in different settings. Crystal says, "Appropriateness in language is the same as appropriateness in other walks of life. Take clothing. If you looked into your wardrobe and found there only one suit of clothes, or only one dress, how prepared would you feel to face the sartorial demands made upon you by society?" You don't wear a swimsuit to a job interview, just as you don't wear business attire to the beach or when gardening.

Prescriptive grammarians assume that we need only one set of rules to cover every occasion. To the extent that is true, it is more applicable to standard English. Yet much of our word-usage is informal: in speech with friends or family, emails, texts or in other settings, for which more relaxed rules apply. Yet even these less formal settings have rules that command our

---

[91] Gordon S. Jackson, *Never Say "Moist" at Wyndover College.*

attention. Crystal says, "Every sentence we speak or write involves a choice. We hope we have made the right choices— that we have chosen language which is both meaningful and acceptable to our listeners and readers."

Ultimately, how we speak and write is a synthesis of all these choices, a synthesis that reveals our characters. As Harry Emerson Fosdick puts it, ". . . our words show where our souls have been feeding." May our words match the people we aspire to be.

Acknowledgements

I owe thanks to several friends who provided feedback on drafts of this manuscript. They include Ted Ketcham, Leslie Smith, Lily Winslow, and Jeff Haschick—who has generously given of his time in commenting on several of my books. As always, my family—Sue, Sarah and Matthew—provided input that helped me to strengthen the book.

Even though they are no longer with us, I must recognize my parents, Stanley and Myrtle Jackson, who nurtured my early interest in books and the magic of words. It's impossible for me to imagine how my world would be different without that encouragement.

Interesting word, *encouragement*. We borrowed it from Middle French, *encoragement* (see **Borrowed Words**), and it is first recorded in English in 1549. It has an alternative form, *incouragement*, but that's now seen as archaic. In addition.... *"Oh, be quiet."*

About the Author

Gordon S. Jackson is a South African-born educator and author.

He received his undergraduate education in South Africa and his MA at Wheaton College, Illinois. He worked as a reporter and editor on a news magazine in Johannesburg before obtaining his PhD in mass communications at Indiana University. He then taught journalism at Whitworth University in Spokane, Washington, for 32 years before retiring in 2015.

He is the author or compiler of fourteen books (twelve commercially published), including two satirical novels. He is married to another South African, who he says helps keep his accent honest.

Note from the Author

Word-of-mouth is crucial for any author to succeed. If you enjoyed *Meet the Dog that Didn't Sh*t*, please leave a review online—anywhere you are able. Even if it's just a sentence or two. It would make all the difference and would be very much appreciated.

Thanks!
Gordon S. Jackson

We hope you enjoyed reading this title from:

www.blackrosewriting.com

Subscribe to our mailing list – *The Rosevine* – and receive **FREE** books, daily deals, and stay current with news about upcoming releases and our hottest authors.
Scan the QR code below to sign up.

Already a subscriber? Please accept a sincere thank you for being a fan of Black Rose Writing authors.

View other Black Rose Writing titles at
www.blackrosewriting.com/books and use promo code
PRINT to receive a **20% discount** when purchasing.